PAPER DOG

THE TRUE LIFE STORY OF A VIETNAM WAR DOG

ISBN: 978-1-943492-58-9 (Hardback)
ISBN: 978-1-943492-62-6 (Soft Cover)

Book design by designpanache

ELM GROVE PUBLISHING

San Antonio, Texas, USA
www.elmgrovepublishing.com

Elm Grove Publishing is a legally registered trade name of Panache Communication Arts, Inc.

PAPER DOG

THE TRUE LIFE STORY OF A VIETNAM WAR DOG

JOHN B. KUBISZ, DVM

TABLE OF CONTENTS

Dedicated to Paper, his best friend Tom Hewitt
and the Men of the Fightin' 764th

FOREWORD

*By Ron Werneth, military historian
and former Vietnam Dog Handler Association Historian.*

SINCE THE BEGINNING of time, mankind has had a symbiotic relationship with dogs. This relationship is extraordinary; one based on the undying devotion and unbreakable bound of a canine to his human counterpart. It is easy to understand how dogs, with their intelligence, devotion and high-level of physical senses of smell, vision and hearing, could play an essential role in military combat. The pinnacle of the military use of canines in combat would be in the Vietnam War where they would be credited with saving 10,000 American casualties.

Paper Dog is the story of lifelong veterinarian Dr. John Kubisz, his combat tour in Vietnam and the powerful chronicle of an Army scout dog handler Tom Hewitt and his K-9 partner "Paper." This dog, written off for dead, defied the odds to recover after being severely wounded, recovered then returned to combat. However, this miraculous recovery would have never occurred without the medical support of Dr. Kubisz, his small but skilled team of the 764th Medical Detachment and the love & care from his handler Tom Hewitt. Dr. Kubisz shares his experience of being a young veterinarian from Hammond, Indiana, sent to the front lines of Vietnam. There, in a little, well-equipped clinic at Cam Rahn Bay, he and his men were responsible for the veterinary care of war dogs, from preventive treatments to surgeries; they did everything required to fulfill this duty. *Paper Dog* is a gift to anyone who loves dogs or has any interest in learning more about the Vietnam War as told in the unfiltered and unique perspective of a veterinarian who served in combat.

How this remarkable book came about is a good tale by itself. Over ten years ago after watching a documentary called *War Dogs: America's Forgotten*

Heroes, my life changed forever. In this film, both Dr. Kubisz and Tom Hewitt shared their first-hand experiences of working with canines and the moving story of the dog closest to them, Paper. After seeing *War Dogs*, I embarked on trying to meet and record the stories of these unique Vietnam veterans and heroic dogs before they were lost to time.

Remarkably, after searching for several years, I located Dr. Kubisz in Lafayette, Indiana, still working as a veterinarian over 50 years later. When we spoke I learned about his yet unpublished book manuscript that was written over thirty years ago and needed to be published. Ultimately, this led to the book you are now reading getting finished and shared with the world. The images in this work are likewise treasures, many of which have never been seen before. I am honored and delighted to have played a small role in helping this special project become a reality.

Paper Dog shines new light on the contributions and sacrifices of both human and four-legged Vietnam veterans.

PREFACE

IT IS HARD FOR ME to believe that it has been 50 years since I was introduced to Paper. I've been a veterinarian since 1967. Of course, I have always loved dogs, loved reading about them and have had many that I always thought were the best dogs in the world. However, there is a story that most people have never heard and remains the most extraordinary dog story of my life!

A lot of movies have been made and many books have been written about Vietnam but there is hardly a mention of the contribution made by the war dogs of Vietnam – a group of canine heroes numbering in the thousands. I recently visited the Vietnam Memorial in Washington D.C. Looking at the immense wall with over 58,000 names, I found myself wondering how much longer this wall would be if we didn't have the war dogs. Around 3,800 served. Only 232 returned!

Most of us would rather forget that war, but for those who lived through it, that's impossible. This is a story that takes place in Vietnam but it's a story of love and devotion that may have happened anywhere. It's the love of a boy for his dog and a boy who became a man too quickly in a hostile environment.

There are only a few left who can tell the complete story of the dogs in Vietnam. As the commanding officer and veterinarian of the first evacuation hospital serving I and II Corps, I feel that I saw the war from both sides. The courage shown by the scout dogs, sentry dogs, and their handlers is a story that should be told.

Paper was the kind of dog you read about in books. However, unlike most dogs in books, he was a real hero despite being named Paper. I've told his story many times to my friends and family and as many times as I have told it, it is still exciting. Every morning when I enter my office at work, a picture of Paper greets me, looking down from the wall.

This book is not only Paper's story, it is also mine. I hope the reader isn't bored, but I feel I must set down the amazing events that brought us together. How did a kid from a poor neighborhood end up being a veterinarian in Vietnam? I realize that, by today's standards, my book is not politically correct and I apologize, but the words, phrases and dialogue are accurate for 1969.

It was two years of my life that changed me forever. I still wake in the middle of the night and I'm back in 'Nam. The images, people, smells and stories are burned into my memory forever. I can almost reach out and touch them.

JOHN B. KUBISZ

Early days.1961 Hammond High School graduation photo.
I was working for a vet in Gary, IN (Dr. Okone).

I.

From the Halls of Purdue
to the Shores of Cam Ranh Bay

It was 1967 and I was graduating from vet school. What a time to live – the Beatles, the Beach Boys, the Rolling Stones and Buck Owens and the Buckaroos; draft card burning, student protests – Vietnam!! The very word strikes at the very core of every American. It was a time that will never be equaled in our country's history.

When I graduated from Hammond High School in 1961, everyone thought that the war would be over pretty quickly, but the reality that I might end up in Vietnam hung over me and my family. I grew up on the tough northside of Hammond, Indiana, where I think everybody would have been considered poor by today's standards, but we never felt poor. My father worked 43 years at Inland Steel in East Chicago, Indiana. He was a prince among men and one of the few "men" that I ever knew in my life. My mom worked for the Queen Anne Candy Company and was that special Polish mom, living to cook enormous meals for her family, friends, relatives and the Chicago Bears if they happened to drop by. Together on a modest income, they were able to raise my sister, Charmaine, and me and send us both to college.

I always hated school for as long as I could remember. My true love was animals and I spent many a great summer on my aunt's farm in Hartford, Michigan with the dogs, cats, cows, horses and all the wild critters. When I was 11 years old, I operated on a turtle that had some kind of growth on his head. I got some ether, put it on a cotton ball and covered his nose until he was limp. I used my mom's manicuring scissors, cut it off and placed some penicillin ointment on the wound. The operation was a complete success. I was hooked forever. I had to be a veterinarian.

To help with expenses, I worked my college summers at Inland

Steel with my father in the Yard Department. My father never finished high school, but he knew the importance of a college education more than I did. Working a summer at the Number 3 Open-hearth Furnace, Inland Steel will give anyone who wants to drop out of high school or college an instant crash-course on the importance of education.

I made it through pre-vet and into vet school in two years. I didn't want to spend any more time than necessary in school or the steel mills. By my second year of vet school, Vietnam loomed larger than ever. An Army recruiter talked to our class about their early enlistment program. You could be commissioned in vet school and then enter the Army as a captain with two years seniority. It could still mean Vietnam but since I was destined to end up being drafted anyway, why not make a few extra bucks?

It was becoming increasingly popular to disagree with the war but I never felt that anyone should ever give an opinion if you didn't know the whole story. Men were dying over there and you would be better to keep your mouth shut. Even today, I resent so-called "activists" like Jane Fonda who spent their time kissing up to the commie back-stabbers when Americans were dying for our country. Where was she when millions were killed by these same people in Cambodia after we left or when Russia invaded Afghanistan? I guess deep inside I wanted to go, if for no other reason than to quell my curiosity. So I graduated from the School of Veterinary Medicine at Purdue University. I was officially a Doctor of Veterinary Medicine and a captain in the United States Army! It wasn't bad for a kid who hated school all his life. Goodbye Purdue and goodbye to school forever. I was single and free at last! Before officially being commissioned, I had to go to Chicago for your basic Army physical. Standing around naked all morning in some dirty, drafty warehouse with some iced-fingered clown poking my unmentionables is not my idea of having a good time. But, I turned my head, coughed a few times and passed. If I would have kissed the guy, I could have avoided the military entirely. We were issued uniforms and instructions to pack our bags for beautiful Fort Sam Houston in San Antonio, Texas.

Fort Sam was the school for basic training of doctors, nurses, dentists, and veterinarians. It was a joke. It meant six weeks of shining shoes, marching, learning to salute and crawling through barbed wire in 110 degree heat. It was the Army's way of showing you a good time. I had never been that far south before and I thought I was going to cook my gonads off! For six weeks, the temperature never fell below 100. I concluded that it was some kind of preparation for Vietnam.

I could never get into the Army's regiment and discipline. I was just starting to have fun being out of school and here I was in another school where I had to wear a uniform, march and salute everything that wasn't painted.

The veterinarians numbered thirty-five and our platoon leader was a Korean War veteran who was lucky enough to be redrafted as a veterinarian when he was 35 years old (the maximum age they were drafting anybody). He wasn't going to play soldier any longer and was determined to give the Army all the grief they wanted. Marching past the WACS in the morning drills, he would give the command, "Eyes… right" and then look at the WACS and yell, "Adjust… Straps!" How could any of us take this BS seriously?

Camp Bullis was the weapons and obstacle course for Fort Sam. I was basically a small animal-minded person but being 6'3" weighing 210 pounds, and wrestling cows and horses through vet school was all the practice I needed for this Mickey Mouse training. I thought the doctors and especially the dentists were all going to die! They would always finish last which was way behind the slowest veterinarian. They were constantly getting hung up in the barbed wire and some of them damn near drowned, crawling through puddles when live ammunition was being fired over their heads. How they were ever trusted with weapons and real bullets was another question. All of us had to show some proficiency at handling an M-16 rifle and a .45 caliber pistol but the Army instructors had to be getting hazardous duty pay.

"Now, gentlemen," the instructor would proudly announce with authority, "Lock and load your weapon." He'd calmly wait. "Ready… aim… fire – at the targets, at the targets!" He was quickly out of the line of fire.

I'm sure the instructors were under pressure to see that everyone passed – when the going got tough, they gave up trying. After all, it had to be better than in Vietnam.

Once in a while, we got a two-day pass to see the sights. At that time, the only thing of interest to me was the Alamo. I was never much for history, but it was still impressive. A few of us decided to make a trip to Nuevo Laredo on the Mexican border since we were only 100 miles away. The trip down showed us the rest of southern Texas – miles and miles of nothing but miles and miles. Mexico is truly the land of opportunity if you happen to be a cactus! We visited the infamous "Boys Town," a Mexican brothel that offered everything you wanted and a few things you didn't need.

After Fort Sam, we were shipped back to Chicago to the Army's School of Public Health. We spent another month sitting in stuffy classrooms learning the difference between pork chops and chicken. I couldn't believe this crap (for the lack of a better word). I went six and a half years to vet school to save animals' lives and now I'm looking at a parade of dangling carcasses in some slaughterhouse — and now, let me see... is this choice, grade A or dog food? Give me a break!

The only way the instructors kept discipline was to constantly threaten us.

"Gentlemen, if you do not learn this material, you will not get a good duty assignment like Captain Smyth. You will not pass GO and will be sent directly to Vietnam; or worse, you will be sent to Greenland with Captain Kubisz!"

I couldn't wait for my first duty assignment. I was sure it would be Vietnam. It was worse than I expected... Bayonne, New Jersey. Now I was born and raised outside the big city of Chicago, and I thought I was somewhat prepared for Jersey and New York City, but I had no idea. I know many people love the big city but if I had to drive 1,000 miles around it, I would never go back. Attention Midwesterners!! Stay out of this area!

I was an outdoors kind of guy... fishing, hunting, swimming, etc. I loved the fresh air of the North woods. Here, on a clear day in Bayonne, I could almost see my feet. So, my dream of becoming a great small animal practitioner started by inspecting dairies and dairy products from Trenton, New Jersey to New York City. I collected samples from all the businesses that supplied food for the Army and took the samples to the lab in Manhattan for analysis. About the only thing I learned that I can pass on to my readers is to watch for off-brands. A lot were so contaminated with rodent droppings that they could be sold as laxatives. But despite this realm of knowledge, six months in this hole and I wanted out.

The only saving grace in my tour of northern New Jersey was occasionally I would find a trout stream in the back of a dairy farm that I was inspecting and could catch a few fish, but I always wondered if I would glow in the dark if I ate any. Once, I even attempted pheasant hunting. It was shortly after opening day and the hunters were thicker than the corn stalks I was walking through. I scared up a bird and he broke to the left of me. In my direct line of fire was another hunter. I immediately lowered my shotgun but at that very instant, I realized that this guy was going to shoot directly at me. I instinctively hit the ground as bird-shot rattled the corn stalks around me. By the time I stood up to check for wounds and yell a few choice words, the jerk had disappeared. For the first time, I felt like the game I was hunting. I have never been hunting since and this episode was all I needed to say goodbye to New Jersey.

My immediate superior was Colonel McChesney at Fort Wadsworth, Staten Island. He was an all right guy for an Army "Lifer" veterinarian. I could never understand how the Army could keep anyone of his talent. Most officers in the Vet Corps above the rank of captain became an immediate desk jockey, scrapping any remnant of his education and spending the next twenty years of his life, not "making waves," so that he could get his next promotion.

The N.C.O.s (Non Commissioned Officers), sergeants and Spec. 5s ran the Veterinary Corps. They did the footwork and the paperwork. I'm sure most of them resented us snot-nosed kids coming out of college and telling them that their spelling was terrible on their reports. Hell, I was 24 years old and some of these guys were my father's age. The *yes sir*-ing and saluting was a real drag. They would salute us to our faces and give us the one-finger salute to our backs.

I played basketball in the evenings at Fort Wadsworth with the colonel and was on a first-name basis. He seemed surprised that I wanted a transfer. "This will probably mean Vietnam," he warned. "At this point, any place would be better and after a day of hunting in Jersey, Vietnam might even be safer," I replied. "I'll see what I can do. I heard a position is opening in Okinawa. Would you like that?" the colonel asked. "Sure! My old roommate from Purdue is stationed there and it will be party time!" I exclaimed.

About two weeks later, I received my orders for Okinawa. I got on the phone right away and called my folks and my sister and told them not to fear, I'm on my way to Okinawa. Their worries about Vietnam were over and I'm out of Bayonne. Two weeks later I got another set of orders —Vietnam!!

"What the hell happened to Okinawa, colonel?" I asked over the phone. "I've got orders for Vietnam in my hand!"

"I told you that you were going to Okinawa and that's all I know," he answered. "Don't worry about it."

Well, knowing the Army brass screw-ups, it didn't take me long to figure that someone had screwed-up! I called Washington to get the straight poop or as we used to say, the "P.P." – the pertinent poop. After putting me on hold and shuffling me from department to another, the word was final... Vietnam here I come! The position in Okinawa was given to a major who outranked me or kissed the right asses.

The news wasn't a shock to me. Somehow, I knew that I would go to Vietnam. My only concern now was telling everyone back home that Okinawa was canceled. I was sure my mother would be dragged away screaming hysterically... not only was she Polish, but she was also a Pisces (the proverbial worrier of the Zodiac).

"Is there any way my mail could be forwarded through Okinawa so my parents could get all my mail postmarked there?" I asked the general.

"That's not the usual response that someone has when I tell them they're headed for Vietnam, but no, there's no way I could authorize that," the general replied. "Good luck!"

There was no way the Army could screw me up any more than they already had, and I was determined from that time on, to give them as much grief as I could get away with.

Everyone going to Vietnam had a thirty-day leave before departing. I think it was over a week before I could find the words to tell everyone that I was going to Vietnam. My mother started crying, my sister started crying and my girlfriend started crying. My dad, who served in World War II, was a little more in control but I could read his mind. Mom and he worked all their lives just for the kids and now his only son was off to some Godforsaken place that most people couldn't find on a map.

How many families had to face the reality that their son or daughter might be leaving and not coming home? We all had a few weeks to ponder the circumstances. Dad and I went to Canada for a few days. The time we spent on our annual fishing trips was always very special to both of us. My sister, Charmaine, and my mother tried to kill me with food and attention. And then there was my girlfriend, Dee Dee. She was my girl and we had dated on and off for four years. We went to see *The Green Berets* starring John Wayne and her tears were flowing by the time we exited. She was convinced that I would not return from Vietnam and our dreams of getting married and living happily ever after would never happen. Sometimes our lives are guided by forces beyond our control.

I always hated goodbyes, but I knew the one for Vietnam would be a pip. I wanted to just get dropped off and be forgotten, but the mourners lined up with their long faces until the call for final departure was given. My mother, father, sister, Dee Dee and assorted relatives all stood with tears in their eyes. The lump in my throat was the size of a basketball. What could I say? Something stupid like, "I shall return!" I felt the most for my parents, putting up with me for twenty-five years, all their skimping and saving to get me through college. Now, no one had control over my destiny.

"Goodbye mom, goodbye dad! Don't worry!"Around us were many families in various stages of goodbyes to their sons. Hands pulled and tugged at me until I wrestled free and walked the long corridor to the plane like some prisoner on death row headed for the gas chamber.

The planes the Army used to transport us to Vietnam were commercial planes stripped down to hold more people. A plane that was built to hold 150 passengers now could hold 250. How the damn thing got off the ground was a miracle! You talk about no-frills flying, the Army invented it. They served your typical Army meal – a sandwich with one slice of stale lunch-meat between two dried slices of bread and an apple probably picked a year ago. I already missed mom's home cooking.

The plane ride was uneventful. I don't even remember talking to anyone. I think everyone was alone with their thoughts or in some state of shock that they had been ripped away from their security of home and family. Most of the ride was in total darkness but I did get to see Hawaii for thirty minutes at a refueling stop. Ten thousand miles is a long ride even in a jet. Finally, as dawn was breaking, the pilot's voice broke the dead silence.

"Gentlemen, if you look over the right wing, you'll see the coastline of South Vietnam. We'll be landing shortly at Bien Hoa Airbase. Thank you for flying 'Take a Chance Airlines'. Have a pleasant stay and good luck!"

The reality of Vietnam gripped all of us. We had been conditioned by the daily bloodbaths on the six o'clock news. Would we be shot down before we landed? Why aren't they issuing weapons and flak jackets? Will we have to run for cover when the plane lands? The daily news gave us preconceived notions of Vietnam, but no amount of news-watching could prepare you for the reality that *was* Vietnam.

The plane finally landed in the vast wasteland called Bien Hoa... the Army's attempt at a no extra O'Hare, only busier. The enormity of the U.S. effort in Vietnam was no more apparent than at Bien Hoa. It was a beehive or ant colony with thousands of people scurrying all over the place with no particular rhyme or reason. I would find out later that this pattern would be repeated all over Vietnam, only on a smaller scale. There was no logic to anything done in Vietnam.

I was greeted at the airbase by an old friend, Jack Crawford, a fellow veterinarian who went through basic with me and was stationed in Manhattan while I was in Jersey. At one time he lived on 72nd Street in an apartment building that was inhabited by 70% stewardesses. It was party time from Friday night to Sunday at Jack's place. He was from Dallas and a Texas Aggie but we seemed to get along anyway. When we were in New York, we finagled a free trip to Puerto Rico for working on some admiral's cats.

It was good to see a friendly face. We shook hands.

"Crawford, you son-of-a-gun! Where's the party and what am I doing here?"

"I just hope you're stationed here in Bien Hoa with me," he moaned.

"Nobody should have to suffer this happy horseshit alone!"

Long Binh, just outside of Bien Hoa, was the headquarters for most of the operations in South Vietnam. Crawford was under the constant scrutiny of the upper brass, always having to shine his jungle boots, starch his jungle fatigues and do their every bidding. He hated the Army almost as much as I did, and he had to spend his time watching his hair grow. It was agony for him, especially without a stewardess on his arm.

We got into a jeep and drove a couple of miles through military installations and to the main Army terminal. Jack escorted me to the office of a full-bird colonel in charge of assignments. Crawford waited outside the office as I entered, came to snappy attention and threw the colonel my best salute (lifers always like that kind of stuff).

"Captain Kubisz reporting for duty, sir!!"

What a bunch of bull crap, I thought, but I learned to play their games. After all, who wants to offend some Napoleon who has control of your life? I could tell he was impressed.

"At ease, captain," he returned my salute. "Let's see where in the hell I'm going to send you," as he looked at a map of South Vietnam with a bunch of pins in it. "These pins represent all the veterinarians in-country right now... about 35, I think. Most are food inspectors."

Oh boy! I came 10,000 miles to listen to some jerk tell me that he doesn't know where I'm going. I already knew that most of the vets stationed in Vietnam spent most of their time as food inspectors. So, why in the hell did they need me?

"How about Hammond, Indiana?" I blurted out.

"We would all like to go home, captain, but there's a job to do over here," he replied as he continued studying the pin filled map. I thought to myself... this guy is taking me seriously. The Army has either successfully made him their Manchurian Candidate or he is one of those "Vietnam Wackos" I heard about. Maybe I'll be just like him in a couple of months. God save me!

"Let's see. We have Captain Arihood up at Da Nang, Captain Hoffman at Pleiku, Holmgren at Cam Ranh Bay. Oh yes, Captain Holmgren. That reminds me," he continued. "We're building a new evac hospital for the war dogs at Cam Ranh and I could move Holmgren to that position. He's the port vet right now. How'd you like to replace him as the port vet of Cam Ranh Bay?"

Ray Holmgren was another old friend. When I was in vet school at Purdue, he was my senior partner when I was a junior. We both had the same sense of humor...Jonathan Winters. It was only natural to follow in his footsteps. If Ray could do it, well, so could I and we would be stationed only a couple miles apart.

"Sure!" I said (like I had a choice). What the hell is a port vet? I thought.

"Well, that was easy. Get your gear together and head for Cam Ranh. Captain Crawford!" He yelled through the door. "Get Captain K. off to Cam Ranh Bay. Good luck, captain!"

In a short time, this clown had forgotten my name, and in a little while would probably have forgotten me forever. Everyone had trouble pronouncing my name. The "z" always threw them. It's pronounced without the "z" – *Ku-bis*. But I ended up being called Captain K, Doctor J or Kubi by most of my friends.

"Yes, sir!!" I saluted, did a snappy about-face and exited.

"You lucky shit!" Crawford mumbled. "I'm going to be stuck with these ass-wipes forever. He could have sent me instead."

"Well, some of us have it and some don't," I joked. "I can see that the colonel has taken a strong liking to you, Jack!"

"Kiss my ass! This is really a bunch of bull pucky! Well, maybe we could go on R&R in a couple of months, Kubi – if I'm not bored out of my gourd by these jerks before then!" Jack concluded as I boarded a C-130 for Cam Ranh Bay.

The C-130 was a flying boxcar or flying coffin, depending on how you looked at it. In fact, a few coffins accompanied us on our flight to Cam Ranh. I could see by looking at the other G.I.s around me it didn't take long to have your senses dulled to the seriousness of this war. There wasn't any way to get around in this country except by air. Even a distance of a few miles was almost impossible by a jeep. Cam Ranh Bay was just over 100 miles northeast of Saigon and on the coast. The flight was usually short and safe. The long overseas trip and the constant drone and vibrations of the giant C-130 engines had managed to put me asleep. I was awakened by a tap on my shoulder.

"Look out the window, captain," a voice told me.
I quickly looked through the small window and saw we were just above the waves. What the hell is happening? Are we crashing? What the hell did I miss while I was asleep? My mind raced as I looked around for a life jacket and a way out. Then, someone lowered himself out of the cockpit.

"Relax, gentlemen," he loudly announced. "We're just practicing emergency ditching procedures!"

"Practice your damn ditching procedures on your own damn time, mister, without a bunch of passengers on this flying piece of shit!!" I yelled out, almost surprising myself.

It didn't take long for most guys to learn not to take any crap over here. Your life could depend on it. What else could the Army do to you? Send you to Vietnam? Maybe if I wasn't an officer the flyboy would have ignored me, but taking one look at the railroad tracks on my lapel this clown jumped back into the cockpit and the plane climbed quickly. There was faint applause and mutterings.

"Damn straight, captain!"

"Stick it to 'em, captain!"

Just before heading to Vietnam. I was young and very green.

II.

Vietnam Vet

FROM THE AIR, I could see Cam Ranh Bay sticking out from the mainland. It looked like the Indiana Dunes State Park back home. There was brush, rolling hills and long stretches of beautiful beaches. Army and Air Force installations dotted the ten mile long peninsula. A large port area was to one side with many ships docked in it. Cam Ranh Bay had one of the best natural harbors in the world and was the main port of entry for supplies to I and II Corps.

Ray Holmgren was there to greet me as soon as I stepped off the C-130. He was grinning from ear to ear as he got down on all fours and started bowing. I thought he had found a new religion.

"Thank you, thank you, there is a God!" he was yelling as I walked towards him.

"It's that bad, huh, Ray?" I shook his hand.

"Oh, it's worse than that, John!" Ray answered. "Another day as a port veterinarian under these assholes at the 176th, and I'll be in Ward 8!"

Ray had been the port vet for six months and was attached to the 176th Vet Detachment. This was a full-fledged vet unit headed by a colonel; under him was a major; five or six vet captains; one or two lieutenants; 30 to 40 enlisted men. These units were so tied up in red tape, paperwork and the proverbial Army SOPs (Standard Operating Procedures), it was a miracle that anything got done. Ray was being transferred to a newly constructed evacuation hospital for the war dogs on Cam Ranh. He would no longer be assigned to the 176th and would be completely on his own as the C.O. of the 764th Medical Detachment. He would actually be a real veterinarian taking care of sick and injured dogs.

I spent the seven mile jeep ride from the Air Force Base to the

Army Base listening to Ray moan and groan about the job I was getting.
As we approached a collection of wooden buildings, Ray was still high with
enthusiasm.

"This is the BOQ," Ray announced. "This is where you'll be
sleeping for the next year; a thing of beauty, huh?"

BOQ stood for Bachelor Officer Quarters. They should have been
called BBOQ (Beyond Belief Officer Quarters!). They were constructed of
unfinished lumber on a concrete slab. Screens covered most of the front and
back walls and two officers shared a 12 x 12 foot room. There wasn't any
running water at all, but a central latrine area where there was a cold water
shower – when there was any water at all. Hundreds of officers occupied a
dozen rows of these two-story buildings. Sand surrounded everything with
very little vegetation apparent. The heat and humidity were worse than at
Fort Sam. Everybody moved in slow motion in jungle fatigues that drooped
like wet tissue paper. Any breeze kicked up sand that clung to your skin and
got into your eyes.

Ray escorted me to my room assignment, and I knew he was gloating
at my expression of disbelief and bewilderment, although I thought I was
hiding it pretty well.

"Don't worry, Kubi!" Ray quipped. "You'll get used to it… the sand,
the flies, the roaches, the Army pancakes!" He laughed as he got into his jeep
and drove away.

My assigned roommate also graduated from Purdue with me but
was married and already in a routine of the living dead. He had little to say
and spent every waking hour writing letters home and reading books. I never
had much to say to him when we were in school and now even less.

"What do you do around here for excitement?" I asked.

"There isn't anything to do around here except write letters and
read. You'll go out of your mind here, Kubisz. There aren't any broads,
either," he said sarcastically.

I was a Purdue Playboy, with a love 'em and leave 'em reputation. It
was greatly exaggerated. At Purdue, I lived in a house with four other guys,
all single. Outside of us, everyone in the class was either married or spoken
for. We all got a reputation for partying and womanizing. My new roommate
was making an attempt at lowering my ego and placing me in the same rut
that he had accepted.

Your first night in Vietnam is unforgettable, especially when you're transplanted from the sterile confines of the United States. Even a ghetto slum would have been an improvement over these wooden shacks with a single light bulb hanging from the ceiling. And this was certainly the best housing in Vietnam. The enlisted men surely had it worse, especially if they were in the boonies. You can bet the Vietnamese had it worse. Some lived in cardboard boxes and lived off the garbage we threw away. I often thought that the complainers in the United States should spend a year in a country like Vietnam.

I lay there only in my Army green boxer shorts, sweat rolling off my face and chest. I listened to the scratching and scurrying noises… probably the mice fighting the roaches for the canned goods. Earlier that afternoon, I opened a box-like chest and was greeted by huge flying roaches. Vietnam had every kind of cockroach from the common crawling Indiana Harbor variety to the giant, flying Viet Cong roaches! Every type of creeping, crawling and flying critter that ever existed was alive and well in Vietnam. Every once in a while, the sweat that I thought was rolling down, began to roll back up! I'd wipe or swat to find a roach or spider. Even to this day, I can't stand the feeling of sweat rolling off my body.

I quickly got into a routine of preparing my bed for sleep. First, I would shake the sheet free of sand and bugs. Then, I would shake the lumpy mattress and pillow and replace them all. The iron spring excuse for a bed was a little more comfortable and free of sand, and it gave me somewhat more security that the bugs wouldn't carry me away by morning.

Strange and unusual odors constantly filled the air. Nothing, not pictures, movies or books could ever convey the smell of Vietnam. Everything had a smell, usually obnoxious. Your own clothes were never completely dry and a host of molds and mildews and body odors created your own macho fragrance. If the breeze was blowing in the right direction, the latrine odor dampened your desire for breakfast, lunch or dinner.

Hours would pass as I lay wide awake. My mind was racing trying to comprehend and adapt. It was Saturday night. Back home I'd be parked somewhere with Dee Dee in my new 1967 442 Oldsmobile that I bought before going to New York. I was single and the Army was giving me enough spending money to make life interesting. What the hell am I doing here? I'll survive. Others did it. I can do it. I'm in a fairly secure area… Cam Ranh —

"AGGGHHH!!!!!!" A blood curdling scream pierced the thick night air.

"What the hell was that?" I yelled out, my feet hitting the cool concrete floor. I ran outside into the darkness.

The scream was just a short distance away to the back of my room in the area of the latrine and showers. I ran back and around the building. The noise and confusion were enough to wake the entire BOQ. As I approached, someone was shining a flashlight in some guy's face who looked like he'd seen a ghost. He had a towel wrapped around him.

"Are you alright?" someone asked.

"Shit!" he yelled. "I went to take a shower and was feeling around for the pull-string and I pulled a huge fucking lizard's tail and it fell on my back. A God damn, fucking lizard, the size of fucking Godzilla. I'll never go in the fucking shower at night again!!"

There was laughter from one end of the BOQ to the other. The tension was broken and I returned to the room and finally managed to sleep. I awoke the next morning to a beehive of activity. Looking from the doorway I could see a bunch of Vietnamese girls and women scampering around with heavy loads of laundry in their hands. These were the *Mama-sans*. Each was assigned from five to seven officers to wash their jungle fatigues daily, shine their boots and clean their rooms. Clothes were washed by hand in large aluminum pans and hung out to dry on ropes. The *Mama-sans* would then squat on the concrete floors and iron them on an old Army blanket.

"Good morning, *Dai Uy* (Vietnamese for captain)!" A friendly face popped in my doorway, "I'm your *Mama-san*. I do the number one job for you! My name Mai. What you name?"

"John," I replied.

"John," she echoed. Number one name. I take good care you, *Dai Uy* John," as she busily gathered up my clothes and carried them off.

Mai looked like she was in her late 30s but I found out later she was only 24. The Vietnamese assigned numbers to everything… the number one was the best and the number ten the worst. So, Mai was kind of Bo Derek in reverse. The hardships of these people became immediately apparent. These girls and most of them were just girls, performed back-breaking labor for about $75 a month, seven days a week, no vacations, no health benefits, no chance for advancement, and no hope of having anything better. They were my immediate inspiration and I forgot any self-pity I might have been feeling.

As I watched in amazement at the *Mama-sans* working, I could see a steady stream of officers headed across the street to the mess hall. I think the only thing I had to eat in the past 24 hours was that dried sandwich on the trip over. I wondered if Army pancakes were as bad as Holmgren suggested. I got into the line and waited to pick up my metal tray with its various sized compartments.

The Army was never known for the quality of their meals but everything was in abundance. The first stop was a giant platter of yellow, scrambled stuff called eggs. All Army eggs were powered and then water added and they were cooked into something that looked like eggs. But, there was bacon, sausage, hash browns and the ever popular "shit-on-a-shingle" (chipped beef on toast). Then, I saw the infamous Army pancakes! They were about the size of '56 Chevy hubcaps and of equal weight and texture. The coffee looked like coffee, it smelled like coffee, but it tasted more like wild hickory nuts. I took what looked edible and headed for a group of fellow veterinarians.

"Hey, Gang!" Holmgren yelled. "This is my replacement at the port, John Kubisz, call him Kubi," he announced.

We exchanged introductions and complaints about the various aspects of breakfast.

"Hurry up and eat, Kubi," Ray said gulping. "I can't wait to take you over to see the colonel, get you signed up at the 176th and get my ass out of there for good!" he laughed.

"Don't worry, John," someone else said. "It's not the colonel you have to watch out for. It's that asshole major!"

Everyone laughed in agreement and Ray and I headed for the 176th. I reported to a lieutenant colonel named Lamarr. Colonel Lamarr was a pot-bellied laid-back kind of officer content to ride his desk into retirement, hoping someday to reach that magical pinnacle called full-bird. He belched after every sentence. I thought it was the Army pancakes but he said it was some kind of birth defect, an esophageal curvature or something.

The real problem at the 176th was Major Kraft — a short Napoleonic figure with dreams and aspirations of becoming general. The colonel was just a figurehead. Major Kraft was going to show everyone that he was a major! He was a major alright, a major screw-up and a major pain in the ass for everyone. The Army was the perfect place for this type… couldn't command respect in the civilian world, so he got rank in the Army and everybody had to say "Yes, sir" and salute him. He loved giving orders, especially direct orders and going around making sure that everybody had short haircuts, polished boots and pressed jungle fatigues. One look at each other and it was instant dislike. He was everything right with the Army and I represented everything wrong in his world.

At least I didn't have to share the same office with these oak-leaf jerks. The office of the port vet was atop the highest point at Cam Ranh Bay and under the control of the Transportation Command. From my new office, I could look all over the port and most of Cam Ranh Bay.

As I said before, Cam Ranh Bay was fairly secure as Vietnam went. There was an occasional rocket attack or surprise sneak attack but few and far between. Cam Ranh Bay had become a gigantic monument to the spectacular waste of materials, money and men's lives… the largest overseas project the Army ever undertook. Most people picture Vietnam as a war movie of never ending jungle fights and for a few, that's what it was. But, for every man on the front lines, there were 20 men supporting him. At Cam Ranh Bay they totaled 25,000. And, for a lot of these men, even in secure areas, this war was their own private hell.

I use the term "men" loosely. At 25, I was old for Vietnam. Most of these guys were under 20. Looking back, we were all babies. Even at 25, I was poorly equipped to be a Commanding Officer. I always thought that we should have a global Geneva Convention and outlaw anyone under the age of 45 from fighting and if the U.S. goes to war, the people in Congress go first. All wars would end today.

The other thing I couldn't understand was why we were fighting this war as if it was going to continue forever. We didn't build temporary facilities; we built permanent ones, and damn good ones at that. We built good roads and communication systems. Why didn't we all get together and start marching north and kick their asses up to China? 500,000 men committed to this war, or excuse me, "political action," and less than a tenth actually fighting. And, more importantly, they're fighting and dying slowly here and there for what reasons? The best of our country's life blood spilled for what? I never felt that we shouldn't be there, our country made the decision, but let's get the job done and get the hell out! Instead, we had the best fed, the best equipped, most powerful Army in the world sitting around with their fingers up their asses. The buck had to stop somewhere and it was at the top… an inept President and a wishy-washy Congress that worried more about the Jane Fondas and getting votes than they did about our kids dying in Vietnam. In the words of LBJ:

"We hope that peace will come swiftly, but that is in the hands of others besides ourselves and we must be prepared for a long, continued conflict. It will require patience as well as bravery… the will to endure as well as the will to resist…"

And so on and so on… the politicians babbled. Peace was in the hands of no one outside of Washington D.C. and the war could end quickly by putting all the politicians in Vietnam for a weekend. I have always felt that if Kennedy wasn't killed, there wouldn't have been a Vietnam.

Anyway, that's all the editorializing I'll do. But, since I'm writing this, I had to express my views, Jane.

The position of Port Veterinarian was as menial, dull and boring as Holmgren described. The job sucked worse than a toilet plunger with a hole in it. Two enlisted men were assigned to me and our job was to check all the food kinds of stuff entering the port. When a ship arrived, we would check the manifests and board the reefer ships to visually inspect and take samples. If everything was OK'd, the ships were unloaded and the products distributed to holding areas at Cam Ranh for further distribution throughout I and II Corps. Just talking about it now, I'm bored to death!

It was only my second week when a ship arrived and immediately after docking, lost all the power to its freezer. Ninety tons of meat and poultry sat defrosting. All the top brass… generals, colonels, and majors… had an emergency meeting to come up with a solution. I was the only captain invited and I sat quietly in the back of the room listening to the BS fly, thinking to myself that they would soon come to the obvious answer. Why even have this meeting? They're wasting time!

"Where's the port vet?" some colonel asked. "Let's get his input."

Oh, hell. They discovered me. I raised my hand.

"What should we do, captain?"

"First of all, I'd stop flapping your gums and get every available truck and every available man and unload the damn thing before we have ninety tons of garbage!" I said confidently.

The room was silent. Everyone looked at everyone else. A simple solution had presented itself… a solution, unlike an Army solution. I recalled the old expression… there are three ways to do something: the right way, the wrong way and the Army way!

"Can we do that?" one colonel asked another, who shrugged his shoulders.

"OK, captain, we'll give it a try. Everyone cooperates in this effort and give the captain as much help as he needs."

Without wanting to, I became responsible for this entire operation. I don't think anyone wanted the responsibility or was willing to get a black mark on their record if this idea failed. Within the hour, everything with wheels was loaded with meat and trucked over to cold storage. In twenty-four hours, the entire ship was unloaded without even the slightest thawing. All over Transcommand, everyone was buzzing that I had engineered this plan that saved the Army thousands of dollars. It was my first feather and from that day on I had only my two enlisted men doing most of the work. I found other things to amuse myself.

I volunteered – yes, volunteered – for anything to do with animals. I joined a medical aid and assistance team that helped the Vietnamese. Anytime they had a sick pig or water buffalo, I went to treat it. What the hell did I know about water buffaloes? Not much, but everything seemed to respond to good old penicillin. I hated riding in those Huey helicopters but it was the only way to get to most of these places. They would give us a location and we would fly around it a while looking for *Charlie*.[1] I'd only treat water buffaloes that were already half dead and lying in the field. They were easy to spot. It was almost impossible to handle any water buffalo that had much life in him. Once we landed, three or four infantry types would surround me and the patient and I'd make my quick diagnosis.

"He's sick!" I'd announce. "I didn't spend six years in college for nothing!" I'd give a massive dose of Pen Strep (a common antibiotic at that time) and jump back into the chopper.

Almost everything made a complete recovery and I became more in demand. Being a live target in an open rice field was not my idea of fun. Besides the VC (Viet Cong[2]), the typical Vietnamese water buffalo hated Americans as much as our dogs hated them. The ones left standing were as dangerous as a loaded weapon. On one occasion we had to shoot one that charged us.

Rabies was rampant all over Vietnam. After you've seen children dying from rabies, you'll never forget how deadly and miserable this disease really is. I helped organize a rabies control program, vaccinating everything we could catch and exterminating everything else. We developed a unique way of identifying the dogs we vaccinated since most of them didn't have collars and we didn't have tags. We spray-painted the light-colored dogs black and the dark colored dogs white.

I even got involved with some real exotic critters including Asian elephants, tigers, monkeys and an assortment of reptiles. At least I felt for the first time that I was finally starting to contribute something by working on these assistance teams. As I wrote home in one of my letters, I didn't feel that this was a war of democracy versus communism, but a war to let people have the freedom to decide for themselves what they wanted. This became very clear to me when I visited two islands off the coast of Vietnam.

One island was under the control of the South Vietnamese, the other was dominated by the VC. On the first island we visited, the people were friendly, cooperative and welcomed us and our help. The children were like kids everywhere... laughing and playing. They invited us to eat with them and seemed to genuinely appreciate our efforts.

I was waiting close to the shore for the PT boat when I was approached by one of the village leaders and our translator. He wanted to thank me for the help. When we were on these missions, we all carried an M-16 and officers carried a .45 side arm. The village leader wanted to see my M-16. The translator told me it was alright. Looking back, I would never do it again, but I was young and dumb. I wasn't that dumb to give him a loaded weapon, so I pulled the bullet magazine, cleared the weapon and handed it to him. He looked it over.

"Number one Boom Boom," I dumbly proclaimed.
Both of them burst into laughter. Apparently, I just used the Vietnamese slang for having sex. He handed the M-16 back and I was on my way.

On the second island, within sight of the first island, the difference was night and day. The people refused all help. The animals were hidden from view. The children were dirty, unhappy and in great need of medical attention. But, all efforts were refused. I felt any minute that I would be shot. We finally decided to leave when a little boy came running up to me with a scraggly kitten. I only saw two cats while in Vietnam... in a lot of places, they were part of the diet. The little boy held the skinny kitten up to show me a cut around its hind leg. I remembered seeing a cut like that before and reached into my medical kit for a pair of forceps. Placing the forceps deep into the cut, I pulled up a rubber band that had managed to work its way through the skin and cut completely around the leg. I cut it free and placed some antibiotic ointment into the wound. By now, a small crowd had gathered and was watching. I showed the rubber band to the small boy and shook my finger at him, the universal parental warning, and everyone gave a slight smile or laugh. The little boy held tightly to his kitten and ran away. They were the only smiles that day.

One of the many traits the people of the United States have, that I found greatly or wholly lacking in places like this VC island, was compassion. Protesters can label us invaders or Yankee imperialists or whatever other names they want to place on us. But, wherever we are or wherever people are hungry or sick, we try to help them. On these medical aid and assistance teams, most of the Vietnamese people they visited never saw a doctor or a dentist in their lives. They certainly didn't know what a veterinarian was. Most of them didn't know the Vietnamese word for a veterinarian *(bac si thuy)*. They thought I was a young human doctor practicing on animals until I got good enough to practice on people. This might have been a whole new concept in U.S. medical training!

Every day that I wasn't working with the Vietnamese people seemed the same and I lost track of even the day of the week, except when Monday came. Monday morning was the infamous malaria pill day. It was offered before breakfast and left most guys including myself inside out by evening. Now, I was used to outhouses since my days on my aunt's farm in Michigan, but these suckers were ten-to-fifteen hole Taj Mahals. Under each hole was a 50 gallon drum cut in half. Each morning they were pulled out, mixed with kerosene and burned.

By Monday evening, you practically had to take a number to take a crap. By the time your diarrhea stopped, it was time to take another pill. Some guys made it part of their weekly rituals, sitting on the crapper reading and socializing with the guy next to him.

"How's it goin' Joe-Bob?" grunt, grunt.

"Fine, Billy-Jo," groan, groan.

A couple of weeks of this and I stopped taking my malaria pills for good. I tried to fill my days the best I could but the nights were long, hot and boring.

I vegetated with the zombie I had for a roommate, writing letters to Dee Dee and to my folks. After about two weeks, I was quite sure that my roommate's prediction of me going crazy would become reality if I didn't do something soon. I decided that night to walk out of this wooden coffin and never return.

I walked across the street from the BOQ to a small officers' club. The Army was also building the largest officers' club in Vietnam at Cam Ranh but it wasn't quite completed. This small club had a loud juke box belting out the classics of the era… *Hey Jude, We Got To Get Out Of This Place, I Can't Get No Satisfaction* and *Stand By Your Man*. Out the back door was a miniature version of an outdoor theater… bleachers and a large screen. *Spinout,* starring Elvis Presley was playing. I took a seat at the bar and ordered my usual… bourbon and ginger ale. Beer was ten cents and mixed drinks were 25 cents. It wasn't hard to explain why alcoholism was so high in the military. I started BS-ing with the bar girls. One common thread that the Vietnamese and Orientals share with the Americans is a good sense of humor and the same level of BS.

One particular little girl named Mai became my close friend. Mai was a common name for girls in Vietnam like John for boys in the U.S. I know that every American that went to Vietnam has recollections, feelings, respect or disrespect for the Vietnamese women. Some were hookers and pros only interested in Americans for their money. Others developed lasting loving relationships that progressed into marriage. Here at Cam Ranh, there was a little of both. At the local Vietnamese village, a few bucks could buy you 'a good time', as we called it. I was never much for buying 'it'. My ego always dictated that it should have been the other way around. The girls at the officers' club were more like the girls back home and most were looking for lasting relationships.

There was nothing like what we called 'dating' in 'Nam. Most of the girls in Vietnam were deprived of any normal relationships because of the war. I know it will be difficult for the reader to comprehend or to understand what a relationship was in Vietnam. If you liked someone, what would you do? Ask her out? There weren't any restaurants, movies or dances. You had to make the most of the situation as it presented itself.

Mai was 18 and like most 18-year-old girls everywhere. She was a little young for me but we liked each other's company. It was nothing serious but both of us found some fun in teaching one another English and Vietnamese while studying anatomy by braille.

In the meantime, the job of port veterinarian dragged on and I rarely made an appearance except to sign forms. The only bit of excitement happened on my weekly visit to my desk at the Transcommand. A violent explosion shook the entire office. In the distance, a large cloud of smoke was rising from the ammo pier. This area was isolated because of the dangerous materials and my first thought was that a ship had exploded. Almost immediately helicopters appeared and began shooting into the bay.

I was dock-side when two bodies were fished out of the water. The choppers had managed to make fish food out of them. Apparently, these two VC managed to swim the distance across the bay and attach satchel charges to a ship anchored at the ammo pier. They made it half way back before the charges exploded prematurely. Only minor damage occurred to the ship and no one was hurt.

A South Vietnamese soldier rolled over one of the bodies and found a pouch attached to his belt. He opened it and found a single can of sardines. He calmly opened it, and after wiping the blood from his hands, he ate it with his fingers. People stood around taking pictures like hunters with their deer trophies. As I said, this was a strange world!

One of my grips on reality was helping Holmgren at the 764th. This is what I went to school for – small animal medicine. But, the job at the 764th was a daydream. Holmgren would be leaving in a couple of months and some colonel or major would replace him. Every vet in the country wanted his job and my chances were practically zero. I had also managed to lose all my brownie points with the upper brass at Transcommand over another piece of typical Army BS.

A fire aboard one of the ships had damaged over 100 pallets of beverages, over 1,000 cases of pop and beer. Most of the stuff was still good and still usable. It had been loaded onto a large barge alongside the damaged ship. I asked someone what they were going to do with it and the reply was that they were going to dump it at sea. Not being a wasteful kind of person (the Polish in me), I backed my jeep down the dock and loaded it to the max with about 24 cases of beer. I then drove around the base dropping off a case here and a case there to all my friends. When I got back to my room, I had only four cases left and a message to call Major Kraft's office immediately.

"What's up, major?" I asked.

"I'll tell you what's up, captain!" he growled. "Your ass is in a lot of trouble. An M.P. reported you for stealing beer from dockside. They're looking for you now to arrest you. It couldn't have happened to a nicer guy. Turn yourself in!" he finished and hung up.

Oh boy! I could see the headlines in the *Stars and Stripes* (the military newspaper) – "Port Veterinarian Arrested For Stealing Garbage." I'm a major criminal. I wasn't about to go around and collect all the cases that I already gave away. So, I broke down my four cases into six packs and single cans, stacked them as massively as I could and headed for the docks. I pulled up to the M.P. checkpoint.

"Are you the nice man that reported me stealing this garbage?" I asked the M.P.

"Yes, sir!" the M.P. responded. "I was under orders to look for looters and I couldn't stop you in time, so I had to report you, sir. Sorry about that, sir!"

"Well, Ollie, I'm returning every bit of it back to the barge!" I quipped. "Now, report that!"

"Yes, sir!" he responded. "I'll make sure my C.O. is aware of that, sir!"

I drove the distance down the dock to the barge area about 100 yards away. I stood on the dock about 20 feet above the barge and slowly, practically a can at a time, began throwing the beer back into the barge. As I was unloading, I could see a jeep pull up to the M.P. check-point and I could see that some officer was pointing in my direction and talking to the M.P. that reported me. When I finished unloading, I drove back to be greeted by a full-bird M.P. colonel.

"This is the captain, colonel," the M.P. announced.

"Captain Kubisz, sir!" I gave my best salute.

"I know who you are, captain," he returned. "You're lucky I'm not arresting you right now, but my M.P. tells me you returned it all. Is that correct?"

"Yes, sir! You can search my hooch if you like, sir!"

"That won't be necessary. I know I won't find anything. But, a report will be filed and sent to your superiors. Now, carry on!" he ordered and drove off.

I was wondering who put me on this clown's shit list. Later I found that he was trying to get into Mai's pants when I wasn't around but he couldn't get to first base. This guy was pushing 40. Talk about your dirty old man.

"Sorry about all the crap, sir!" the M.P. apologized.

"This horseshit is what the Army's all about, private. Who's in charge of this dumping operation?" I asked.

"Warrant Officer Carpenter, sir," he replied.

Ted Carpenter was a good friend and also a recipient of two cases of beer that I had stolen. I went back to his hooch and told him what happened and what a damn waste this would be... 1,000 cases of good stuff were being dumped at sea.

"Don't worry, Captain K. When I get done making a few calls, there won't be any waste," Ted replied.

The next day the barge was pulled out from the dock and towed out of the bay around a high point of land called Market Time. Once around this point, it was out of view of the port. Everything from rowboats to destroyers were waiting for it and they descended on the barge like locusts. In less than an hour, nothing remained except empty cans and wooden pallets. The dumping orders were signed: "Dunnage dumped at sea as ordered."

After this incident, I was down to my last brownie point. The Transcommand brass practically looked at me as a common criminal; I was number one on the Major Kraft's manure list, and some M.P. colonel had the hots for my girl and a hair up his butt for me!

It was about this time the Army started shipping all perishables via reefer trucks, piggy-backed on ships from the U.S. They were losing millions because a lot of them came over damaged from freezing or spoiling, especially the lettuce which had a crucial temperature of only a few degrees. No one would claim responsibility; the Army blamed the shipper and the shipper blamed the trucking company. A general staff meeting was called to solve the problem. Uppity-ups from both sides of the Pacific were assembled. BS was once again flying. I wasn't about to get involved in this mess and had almost fallen asleep when I heard my name.

"Captain Kubisz!" a loud voice called opening my eyelids. "Let's hear what you have to say."

I was almost caught flat-footed but I was never one who was at a loss for words. It was time to pull something from the far reaches of the *Twilight Zone*. Brain don't fail me now! I need the points.

"Yes, sir!" I started. "Why don't you have an Army inspector temperature check the vans when they leave California, and when the shipment arrives at Cam Ranh, I'll temperature check and inspect every van within 24 hours and reject any cargo that doesn't meet the requirements. The Army doesn't pay for anything I reject."

I finished and even I was impressed as I looked around the room at the astonished faces.

"It sounds like a lot of work, captain. What would it take to do such a thing?" some general asked.

I really didn't need anything. I could have done the whole project myself. I didn't have much else to do. But, my mind was now in overdrive and the wheels were turning at high speed.

"Well, all I really need is my own jeep and a couple of E.M.s (enlisted men)," I confidently reassured them.

"Hot Dog!! They bought it... hook, line and jeep! The general ordered somebody to get me a jeep and two E.M.s."

"But, general," some lowly major pleaded, "Jeeps are in short supply."

"I don't care, major! This man is going to save the Army millions. Now, if you don't want to lose your own jeep, you'd better find this man one!" the general ordered.

I couldn't believe it. Not many majors or colonels had their own jeep. I created some new jealousies among the C.O.s at the Transcommand and at the 176th. The reefer truck inspection turned out better than my wildest expectations. Just about every day, a ship would arrive, the vans would be unloaded and I'd inspect them. They were loaded with fresh produce and steaks. I stopped eating breakfast at the Officer mess and saved myself for the vans and my own gourmet smörgåsbord. I could eat a fresh apple out of one van or a fresh orange or grapefruit out of another. Some of the vans were loaded with T-bone or rib-eye steaks that required at least one or two to be inspected more carefully over a barbecue.

The smells coming out of every produce van were in sharp contrast to the putrid smells of Vietnam. The pineapples, lettuce, grapes and even the onions were like a breath of fresh air.

With my two men, we could do 100-200 vans in the morning and have the rest of the day to pursue my vet career at Holmgren's 764th or drive to the beach in my new jeep. Besides the obvious benefits to myself, I was saving the Army millions. They couldn't thank me enough... the largest tonnage ever inspected by one man!

"Captain, you're doing a fine job!" the general beamed. "I'm putting you in for at least the Army's Commendation Medal. How else can we help you?"

The general stood there with Major Kraft, Colonel Lamarr and a few upper brasses from the Transcommand. The Army brass was big on medals. All the lifers measured their achievements by the ribbons on their chest like a collection of ornaments on a Christmas tree. I always thought that they should go one step farther and have them blink on and off with colored lights.

"You can give any medals, sir, to my enlisted men. They worked hard for them (and give yourself a few more). I just have one little request," I humbly said. "I don't think I can do any more as port veterinarian. Everything is operational and anyone can do this job now. I'd like to take over as the C.O. of the 764th Medical Detachment when Captain Holmgren leaves next month, sir."

Out of the corner of my eye, I could see Major Kraft squirm as I made my request. All the head honchos were there trying to make brownie points with the general and I was in the front row!

"I think that could be arranged. You're already here and I'll bet you already know the job," the general responded.

"Begging your pardon, sir, we already have several people that have more seniority than Captain Kubisz including a major," Major Kraft meekly interrupted.

Major Kraft thought the job at the 764th was in the bag for himself. "Nonsense, major! The position calls for a captain and no one else is more qualified or has done a better job than Captain Kubisz. Be proud of him, major. He was in your unit!" The general laughed.

You can bet that Major Kraft wasn't laughing or even smiling. Not only wouldn't he get the best job in Vietnam, but, I would be out of his unit and his control entirely. He would, however, from that day on, be like a case of hemorrhoids… a pain in the ass that was hard to get rid of. Within a week I had my orders transferring me to the 764th Medical Detachment. Holmgren was headed home and I would have the job of my dreams.

Notes:

1. *Charlie* or *Mr. Charlie* was the nickname given to the enemy Viet Cong (VC) troops. *Charlie* is part of the military abbreviation of Victor Charlie (VC) when spelled out phonetically.

2. The Viet Cong were the well-armed communist guerrilla fighters who fought against the military forces of the United States and its allies in both South Vietnam and Cambodia. They were a formidable foe who typically tried to fight only in engagements when their chances were favorable, then suddenly disappear into the jungle to fight another day.

III.

The Saigon Warrior

As I said before, Ray Holmgren was a very good friend and he was even more happy than I was about me replacing him… he was going home. The Army always gave a two week overlap period in a change of command so the new C.O. could learn the ropes of the new unit. Ray had the job of a port veterinarian for six months and was the C.O. of the 764th for another six months. During his last six months, I was at the 764th more than Ray was and knew the operation and the men that I was going to work with. Both of us would enjoy a two week in-country R&R. Ray might have been better off if he had left right at that point. A couple of things happened that could have ended with Ray being shipped home in a bag and me with him.

Both of us loved the beach and the shores of Cam Ranh Bay not only had some of the best beaches in the world, but they also had coral reefs with beautiful snorkeling. Rarely was there a surf or high waves. However, during the monsoon season, the waves got up to six or eight feet. We were catching the waves on one of these days as they came around a point of land and body surfing them to the shore. As we continued to catch wave after wave, we began being pulled by currents away from the point of land and far out into the ocean. Before we knew it, we were well over 100 yards from shore and exhausted.

"Can you make it to shore?" Ray asked.

I knew Ray was in trouble. My mind flooded with thoughts. I felt I could make it to shore, but barely. I thought of my days in high school and organizing a scuba diving club, and how thankful I was that we made the test to join so difficult to pass. But, there was no way I could save my best friend. I was torn with the thought of saving myself at the cost of losing my friend. If I tried to pull him to shore, we would both die. I couldn't leave him, but what was the alternative?

"You can't make it, Ray?" I asked, hoping for a *yes I can.*

He was too tired to even answer. He just shook his head in the negative.

"You're going to be alright!" I reassured. "I learned in diving you can stay afloat a long time if you just relax and breathe normally. Try to stay afloat with minimum effort, Ray. I'm going for help. Don't you drown, damn it! You drown jerk-face and I'll kill you. I'll be right back!"

Maybe both of us would have drowned if it weren't for the fact that I left Ray behind. With every ounce of strength and determination, I fought my way through the surf. The waves were breaking before the shore, causing an extreme undertow and washing the sand from the bottom. Even ten feet offshore, I couldn't touch the bottom because of the wash-out. Every time I got close to the shore, I was washed back. Finally, with one desperate last push, I reached the sand and pulled myself out. I struggled to my feet barely able to stand, looking over the waves to see if Ray was still there. My heart practically stopped… I didn't see him. Then, even farther out, I spotted him. I looked up the beach. There were two guys about 75 yards up the beach. I ran or staggered towards them. They looked up in surprise at my frantic face, totally unaware of what was happening.

"Any one of you good swimmers?" I gulped.

"I am!" One responded. "I used to be a lifeguard."

"Well, you're going to need your training and that surf board. You see that head bobbing way out in the bay? He's in a lot of trouble and it will be a bitch to save him!" I continued to gasp.

He grabbed his surf board and we plunged through the waves and past the surf. It was difficult to even see Ray by now, but we continued in that direction. As we approached, we could see Ray was already headed under. He didn't have enough energy to even talk as he clutched the surf board gasping.

"Good job, Ray!" I said confidently. "Let's do this again sometime, huh?"

"Shit!" he gasped. "I don't need this crap. I'm short!"

The three of us spread out the length of the surf board and headed for shore. None of us were willing to let go of our floating security blanket as the waves increased in size and intensity towards the shore. But, as we approached the beach, the breakers again blocked our progress. I finally let go and demonstrated how I made it to shore the first time. I yelled to Ray to catch the top of the next wave and fight through it to shore. We all finally reached the beach and lay face down sucking sand for the next ten minutes. We managed to eventually get up, shake each other's hand and thank one another.

This was Ray's last trip to the beautiful beaches of Cam Ranh. He was going to sit on his hands until his plane was headed stateside. But, again, the boredom caught up with both of us in just a couple days.

"Let's go down to Saigon, Kubi!" Ray blurted out. "They're setting up a second evac hospital for the dogs and I got an extra microscope we could take them."

"I thought we were going to play it safe because you're short?" I remarked.

"Hell! Saigon is safer than Cam Ranh. Those vets down there are sitting on their fingers like us. Let's go party!" he snapped.

Before breakfast, we were on a C-130 headed for Ton Son Nhut Airbase at Saigon. At this time, Saigon was anything but safe. Security was extremely tight and there was an after dark curfew. No one was allowed in or out of city limits without a good reason and military personnel were not even allowed to carry weapons within the city limits.

We landed safely and after asking around, found ourselves at the new evac hospital still under construction about five miles out of Saigon. A small house trailer served as temporary quarters while the hospital neared completion. This hospital would be responsible for the dogs in III and IV Corps. The new hospital would be staffed by two veterinarians. One was from the state of Washington, Chuck Thompson. The other was from Tuskegee University, Bill Walters, the only black veterinarian I've ever known. We sat around exchanging war stories and downing beer after beer.

"Hey, when do we eat around here?" I asked.

"We ate yesterday, Kub, today we drink!" Ray laughed.

"Sure, party it up, Ray. You're short, but some of us have a long way to go!" I answered.

"Why don't you guys take one of the jeeps and drive to Saigon and take in the sights?" Chuck suggested. "Bill and I have to report to some no-mind colonel but we'll be back here about 3:00 and then we can go to the Vietnamese officers' club. It's a blast!"

Neither Ray nor I had ever seen Saigon, so we headed for town.

The M.P.s stopped us at the check point and warned us to be out by dark and not to carry any weapons. Saigon was the largest city in South Vietnam and it would have been a poor excuse for any city in the United States. I remember crossing the bridge over the Saigon River or as everyone called it, the "Saigon Sewer". We stopped to take some pictures. Hundreds of shacks made of wood, bamboo and sheet metal, as far as the eye could see, were built to the river's edge. Some of them were built on stilts over the water. Dozens of sampans with entire families living on them were scattered everywhere. A stench that made your nose twitch rose from this open cesspool that was filled with garbage and human excrement. Occasionally, you would see an animal body floating by and I'll bet, even a human one.

Directly below us under the bridge was a small sampan with a man and woman and two little boys. This was their home, floating in this fetid, fecal soup. The kids were kind of skinny but appeared happy. It was hard to judge their ages. A Vietnamese child that was ten looked like an American child of five or six. But, I'd guess these boys were about eight to ten. Obviously, they were brothers, and like brothers everywhere, were running around this small boat in some kind of game of hit and run. One stopped long enough to take a piss into this septic tank, and at the other end of the boat his brother scooped up a drink from this same sewer.

New Jersey finally started to look like the Garden State. I asked myself, how in the world does anyone survive this mess? It's incredible, with all this adversity staring them in their faces every day, why do they continue? What the hell did these kids do to be born into a world like this? They didn't have a whole lot of choices open to them. If they were the smartest sons of bitches in the world, what hope was there for them? They would work their asses off all their lives and still be on that damn sampan!

We returned to Thompson and Walters' evac hospital about three in the afternoon. Chuck Thompson was complaining that he had to work all afternoon and that evening for the colonel and couldn't continue partying with us.

"Bill, why don't you take Ray and John over to the South Vietnamese officers' club? I'm going to be working all evening with lard-butt!" Chuck relented.

"Yeah!" Bill yelled, "You're going to love it."

We left the trailer and headed up the road a couple of miles to this

Vietnamese version of a night club or 'Boys Town' sitting out in an open field. We knocked at the door and a face appeared at the peep-hole, looked us over and opened the latch. We walked into a cool, almost totally dark room that left us almost blind after being in the bright sunlight. You could hear giggling Vietnamese girls around us and little hands were all over my body.

"Oh, *Dai Uy*! I make you very happy," a voice said.

Before we knew it, we were pulled to the back of the club to a booth. I didn't see anyone else in the entire place but then again, it was almost dark. Walters sat in one booth with a girl he seemed to know. Ray and I sat in another across the table from each other. Before I knew what was happening or could voice any objections, the girl sitting with me had her hands under the table and was giving me a better physical than the Army gave me in Chicago. I thought that any minute she would ask me to cough! Ray sat grinning across the table. His girl was more involved in money negotiations than the one with me who was about to give me a free demonstration.

"Kubi, you dog, you! Ray laughed.

"I'm no pushover, Ray," I managed to say, "but, I can be made!" All of a sudden, Bill jumped up from the other booth, obviously mad as hell.

"Let's get the puck out of here! This broad wants to raise prices around here!" Walters announced. "We'll go to the Mai Lon Hotel tonight and get some good stuff!"

"You're going to have to wait a few minutes, Bill. Kubi can't walk!" Ray chuckled.

"You're so friggin' funny, Ray! I was just getting in the spirit of things," I said, trying to get myself together as the Vietnamese girl kept pulling at me.

"I'm not that kind of guy!" I told the girl as I limply waved my wrist at her and slowly walked out.

"You buy me, Saigon Teas! You big Cheap Charlie!" the girls chanted as we left.

We drove back to the trailer and continued our beer drinking. At about seven, Bill announced that it was time to head for the Mai Lon Hotel.

"I thought the town was off limits after dark?" I asked.

"It is, but that never stops anyone who is in desperate need of a shot of leg! I can always come up with a good excuse to get in," Bill said coolly.

"That's right John! We got an injured sentry dog that needs

immediate attention. I can hear him calling from here. Howoo! Howoo!!"
Ray bellowed.

The lack of sleep and food combined with a dozen beers had
completely wiped out Ray and Bill. I wasn't much better but I must have
known we were headed for trouble as I grabbed my .45 when we left and
tucked it under my fatigues out of sight. One of the sober E.M.s drove us to
the M.P. check-point at the edge of Saigon. Ray and Bill were barely able to
walk up to the M.P.s, a beer still in their hands. We exchanged salutes with
the M.P.s who gave us a dirty look.

"I'm Captain Walters, soldier, and this is Captain Holmgren and
Captain Kubi-Dooby from Cam Ranh. They're specialist-ists-ists!" The
words slurred from Bill's lips.

"That's right, we got an injured sentry dog deep in the heart of
Saigon," Ray continued. "Deep in the heart, deep in the heart of Saigon!!
Doodah, Doodah day!!"

I figured no M.P. would let us drunk skunks through the check-point
but at that moment, some confusion broke out with a bunch of Vietnamese
and the M.P.s moved to stop it. Walters tiptoed right past them, followed
by Ray and me. Before I knew what was happening, we were in a dark
back street of a Saigon ghetto. We didn't walk a block when three bar girls
descended on us.

"*Dai Uy*! You very handsome!" one said to Ray. "I love you very
much! *A yeu em!*"

Then another yelled, "*Dai Uy!*" and it was like ringing the cash
register for the local hookers.

"Man! This is a bad idea, men! Why don't we paint a target on our
asses and grab our ankles?" I asked. "A lot of guys have been killed just being
in the wrong place at the wrong time!"

"You right, *Kemo Sabe!*" Tonto Bill replied. "Let's get the flock out of
here, white man!"

The girls escorted us off the street and into a small apartment
building. Vietnamese music, like you hear in an old Charlie Chan movie,
was playing. We climbed a large circular staircase that opened into a large
studio apartment with a couple of beds and a couch. It was fully equipped
with a television, stereo and bar. Bill Walters and I looked over our girls and
were pleasantly surprised that they were very attractive. However, Ray got a

real bow-wow, not even pick of the litter. He tried to communicate to Bill and me using broken Spanish, French and German that he wanted to leave.

"*Mucho Uggo,* Batman and Robin!" he started.

"*Exito, el pronto. Est* German Shepherd!"

"*Au Revoir! Nein Fraulein! Auf Wiedersehen!*"

"Ray, you dog... you love 'em and leave 'em kind of guy!" I jabbed, trying to get even for that afternoon.

Despite our protests, Ray was determined to leave this beauty queen behind, with or without us. So, before we knew it, we were back on the dangerous streets of Saigon. We took our hats off and turned our collar insignias inward so no one could see our rank. I think the gravity of the situation was beginning to seep in as the alcohol began to seep out.

Then, out of nowhere, appeared a Vietnamese taxi cab that we practically jumped in front of. We stopped it and piled in. These cabs were left over from the French when they occupied the country and were similar to an elongated Volkswagen bug. There was hardly enough room to sit three people. Walters sat in front and Ray and I sat in the back, with me behind the driver.

"Mai Lon Hotel, Amigo." Ray breathed a sigh of relief to be off the streets. "See, no problem! The Mai Lon Hotel is secured for partying all night!"

We drove a couple of blocks when the cab driver looked over at Walters, then at Ray, slowly and carefully.

"*Dai Uy?*" the cab driver asked. "Three *Dai Uy?*" he repeated.

"How the hell does he know we're captains?" I mumbled to Ray.

The cab driver proceeded a couple more blocks like he was in slow motion or had all night. He came to a stop across the street from an open-air market.

"Wait here, wait here! I go get cigarettes," he said in broken English.

"Wait here!"

He proceeded across the street and started talking to the shopkeeper while pointing to the cab. Then, the shopkeeper disappeared. The cab driver grabbed a pack of cigarettes, opened it, took one out, and lit it up.

"Hey! I don't like this crap at all!" I said while Ray and Bill were starting to get in the party mood, totally ignoring what was happening.

"Remember when we were basic and they said if a cab driver ever leaves you alone in a cab, you get out fast?" I continued.

"You've been watching too many John Wayne movies, Kubi!" Ray joked.

"Well, I'll tell you two pilgrims, if a grenade comes into this cab, I'm going to be the first one out!" I said in my best Duke impression and started to open the door on the driver's side.

The cabbie was already half-way across the street. I didn't see anything in his hand and I hesitated as he approached. He calmly and slowly got back into the cab. I got Bill's and Ray's attention enough so they were watching this guy, too.

"See, Kubi," Ray relaxed. "Nothing to worry about!"

"Good American cigarettes," the cab driver said puffing.

All of a sudden, the stillness was broken with the unmistakable sound of automatic weapons… *ack, ack, ack!!*

"Someone's shootin' at us!" Walters' wide eyes beamed over the front seat at Ray and me.

Ack, ack, ack. Bak, bak, bak! Several weapons were now firing.

"VC, VC!! GET OUT!" the cab driver kept yelling.

I had always wondered what I would do in a situation like this and now I would find out. I pulled the .45 from my fatigues.

"Mai Lon Hotel, you bastard! *Di Di Mau!*" I yelled as I jammed the .45 to the side of his head, pushing it over to one side.

It took the driver completely by surprise. He thought he had us pegged as easy, unarmed, sitting ducks. The cab lunged forward, wheels screaming, with a hail of bullets all the way behind us on both sides of the cab.

"This son-of-a-bitch tried to kill us!" Walters exclaimed, immediately sober now.

"What the hell would we have done if you didn't have that .45, Kub?" was Ray's sobering comment.

I continued pressing the pistol to the driver's head until the cab jerked up to the Mai Lon Hotel, which wasn't far away.

"I souvenir you cab ride, I souvenir you, please!" the cab driver kept repeating and bowing as I kept the .45 on him.

"I'd like to souvenir you another hole in your fucking head, asshole!" I said my courage and blood returning to my shaking body. My fear was replaced by anger.

"Leave the muther and let's party," Bill urged.

"I feel like I took the wrong turn and ended up in a James Bond movie!" Ray joked. "He ain't worth the friggin' paperwork, John!"

With my .45 still on him, the cab driver got back into his cab and disappeared into the night. We went to the top floor of the Mai Lon and partied 'til the sun came up, like nothing ever happened.

However, this story began to grow almost as soon as we returned to Chuck's trailer. I thought Bill was somewhere else as he told Thompson how I single-handedly fought off the entire North Vietnamese Army. The story was told and retold to the point of being totally fictitious. One account had me killing dozens and capturing others. I have tried to write the actual facts. I never fired any weapon and never even saw our ambushers. Someone once said that the difference between a fairy tale and a war story was one that starts out, "Once upon a time..." and the other, "This is no shit... !"

Ray and I returned to Cam Ranh that morning and even enjoyed the Army's cooking after not eating for a day and a half. Ray was content to be bored until he went home. Goodbyes were happy at the airport this time. Though I was losing Ray's companionship, he was going home and I was getting the 764th all to myself.

IV.

The Dirty Half Dozen

THE 764TH MEDICAL DETACHMENT was a very unusual unit from every point of view. First of all, it was a medical unit, but the only one in the Army headed by a veterinarian. The Army didn't have a TOE (Table of Organization and Equipment) for an evacuation hospital for animals, but it did for people. So instead of making a new TOE, They simply decided to make it comparable to a medical unit with the same equipment and personnel except that the Commanding Officer would be a captain from the Veterinary Corps. However, this C.O. would come under the direction of the General of the Medical Corps in Saigon. The 176th Vet Detachment at Cam Ranh couldn't issue direct orders, but only make suggestions or report anything that they considered irregular. You can bet that Major Kraft was looking for any irregularities.

This whole unit consisted of slight irregulars. The personnel were all 176th rejects. When a new veterinary type enlisted man came in the country, the colonel and major would look them over and pick out who they thought was the best for the Army. If they were good conduct medal recipients and not trouble makers, they would be no problem to be brain-washed into the major's way of thinking. If on the other hand, they were trouble, fought the Army all the way, were complete individuals, then they were given to the 764th. This very process of selection accounted for the most bizarre unit in the Army, and I fit right in! Hollywood could not have combined a more unusual bunch of misfits and weirdos, and I'm using these terms as compliments. Someone upstairs decided to take a bunch of guys from different backgrounds, from all over the United States, and put them in one unit – "The Dirty Half Dozen!"

First, there was David Dow, a Spec. IV (Specialist 4th Class) known as

"Dinky." The Vietnamese word for crazy in the head was pronounced "dinky dow". He wasn't crazy, just a little different. From Texas, he was six foot, five inches with hair sticking out in every direction like a porcupine caught in a brush fire. He resembled a giant Alfred E. Newman in glasses. He never had much to say but you always got the feeling that he knew something or was aware of something that you weren't. Sometimes he would laugh hysterically all by himself and I'd ask him what he was taking from the pharmacy. Dow was a straight-shooter, however, and was my right-hand man. He had a degree in animal science and was the perfect surgical assistant because we were close to the same height. Anyone shorter had difficulty seeing what I was doing because of the height of the surgical table. I could always count on Dink!

On my left hand, there was Francis Bell, another Spec. IV, nicknamed appropriately "Ding-Dong" Bell. Unlike Dow, "Ding Dong" always had something to say. His sense of humor was only exceeded by his temper which was only exceeded by mine. I think we worked together for about a week before he had to test me in a wrestling match one day when no one was around. We pushed and wrestled around the office until he got a bloody nose and I had a few bruises. I think he wanted to see if I was some kind of wimp officer. His curiosity was satisfied and we became the best of friends from that day on. He could almost predict my next move and was equally good at predicting what a dog would do in the treatment room. In the surgery, he was the gas passer (anesthetist) and I never lost a dog due to his negligence.

Thirdly, there was Richard Terwillerger, known as "Snake" or "Grass" and Snake was into grass! Everyone in the unit only used nicknames in communication. Snake was unusual – no – *the* most unusual person I ever met. Dark complexion with black hair and mustache, he said he was from Ohio, but most of us agreed he was from Venus. Snake had spent some time at the venom lab at Fort Knox, Kentucky and was right at home with any creeping, crawling thing in Vietnam. Snake had snakes scattered all over the 764th in office cabinets, foot lockers and bunkers. Some were poisonous but he assured us that we had nothing to be afraid of. He also collected specimens to send to researchers in the States for identification (he discovered several new species while in Vietnam). He was intelligent though, and made an excellent lab technician. Tucked away in his little hole called a laboratory, no one entered this domain for fear of what they might find. He was content to be hung over his microscope and was the loner of the unit. Everyone knew of his fondness for the weed but he never let it affect his performance during duty hours. He remains the best lab person I have ever known.

Next, there was J.B. Jones from New Jersey. He was the unit's clerk although he was wrapped too tight to be a clerk or even be in the Army. He was the epitome of the term "live-wire," and he wasn't taking anything illegal – he didn't have to! Other people got high to act like J.B. did normally. I never saw him sit still for two seconds. Music was his constant companion. If I didn't let him blast us in the hospital, he played it through his headphones. I still picture him dancing around with those headphones in his own private world, singing "Shu-bop, Shu-bop". His music was a part of our day and became part of my treatment and surgery routine. He'd play whatever music I was in the mood for. We clashed a little at first in our music tastes... he liked the Stones, while I was more Roy Orbison or Jerry Lee Lewis, but we could usually agree on Otis Redding or B.B. King, and of course Janis Joplin! J.B. was never much for the blood and guts of the 764th; I think it made him sick, but his energy was contagious and you never sat around when J.B. was present.

Lastly, there was Frank Porter, the senior ranking E.M. How he got by the 176th and into the 764th was a mystery. He was a lifer, Regular Army with a spotless record. Word had it that he was a spy planted by the 176th to keep an eye on us. We nicknamed him "Granny" because of his mother hen complex. Slightly balding, kind of short and chubby, Granny's job was to keep the men in some kind of Army order and discipline... to get to work on time, shine their boots, eat their oatmeal, etc. He was constantly reminding me that I was supposed to be an officer and that I wasn't following SOP (Standard Operating Procedure) for the unit. When I asked him who wrote the unit's SOP, he would reply that I did. I would have him rewrite anything I didn't like or didn't suit me. You'd think he'd get tired of this constant rewriting, but he never did. I think it was the unwritten SOP of the universe that every Army unit should have someone like Porter. My main job for Granny was to make sure he was up for his next promotion or his appropriate Army medal and he made sure that I didn't forget.

There was immediate chemistry that can rarely be achieved in the work place. All of us were different but connected to a common goal. I never remember anyone complaining. No one was ever late for work. My men stayed in E.M. quarters. Packed together like sardines with no air conditioning and very little entertainment. It was seven days of work, no days off and no holidays. Yet, every day, each of them gave their very best.

There was another person, although not part of the Dirty Half Dozen, who became an important part of my life at this time. As I said before, I had kind of a girlfriend in Mai but it wasn't serious for either of us. One evening I went over to the small officers' club across from the BOQ to talk to Mai. I knew she was avoiding me and I bought her a small heart necklace from the PX (I don't think I paid over $10 for it). I was going to surprise her. I walked into the club and saw her whispering in some lieutenant's ear. When she saw me, I could see the handwriting on her face. I didn't say a word, tried to ignore her and sat at the bar with a buddy of mine, Joe Suderland.

"Looks like Mai has a new main squeeze, Kubi!" Joe poked.

"It was fun while it lasted!" I replied.

"Let's go up to the new officers' club and check out the talent," Joe suggested. "Maybe we can drink our blues away."

We drove up to the new club that was built high on a hill overlooking the BOQ. This was a massive structure housing a large bar area, an auditorium for entertainment, a restaurant and a game room with slot machines. We walked through the crowded bar area and sat at the very left end of the long bar. More than a dozen girls were busily taking orders and serving drinks. I sat nursing my bourbon and ginger ale, feeling down after losing two girl friends in one week.

Dee Dee had written me a *Dear John* letter earlier that week. I didn't blame her for giving up on me. After a few months in Vietnam, my letters home to my parents, sister and Dee Dee had dropped to zero. My parents even contacted the Red Cross to make sure I was still alive. Dee Dee was crushed that I didn't even write. It wasn't any loss of affection or concern for her or my parents, but they lived in an entirely different world. The past didn't exist and there wasn't any future. Only the present was of primary concern and real. We are not in Kansas anymore, Dorothy.

So, I got my *Dear John* letter from Dee Dee. She had found someone else — Jesus. That's right, Dee Dee had become a Jesus freak and told me that we were living a life of sin and degradation... she had seen the light. I guess it was better than turning to drugs or alcohol. By now I had expected it, because I saw so many guys get the shaft from their girls back home.

There was one who was saving himself for a R&R with his wife in Hawaii and when he got there, she told him she was saving herself for someone in the States.

Another guy saved himself for his girlfriend who gave him a dose of the clap on his R&R. Still another who found his wife in a porno magazine circulating Cam Ranh. Being trapped in this prison called Vietnam was torture enough for most of these men without getting bullshit from their women back home.

"Man! Now that's talent!!" Joe exclaimed, shaking me from my doldrums.

I raised my head and looked in Joe's direction. She was something special! One look and I was hooked. She was wearing one of those Vietnamese dresses *(Ao Dai)* all in white that was high at the neck and tight at the waist. The tunic draped over black trousers. Her raven black hair flowed over her shoulders and half way down her back. When she walked across the crowded floor, all eyes followed her. She was one of those unique people that radiated a certain something that attracted you to them. I couldn't even make a comment to Joe. I just stared until Joe began pushing me.

"Hey! Kubi, why don't you go over and introduce yourself?" Joe said.

"Oh sure, Joe! That's a degree out of my class. Somebody has probably beaten me already. Every guy in this joint is falling all over themselves just trying to talk to her."

"You never know till you try," Joe assured. "Now's your chance. She's coming this way. Let's see Captain K in action!"

Everyone had this image of me that I was some kind of a ladies' man, but in reality, I was shy and insecure. I probably wouldn't have ever said a word to her, but for Joe's sake and my reputation I would go through the motions. The closer she came, the more beautiful she was and the more uptight I got. My heart was racing! As she came around the end of the bar, I said to her in Vietnamese that she was a very pretty girl. At least the Vietnamese I learned from Mai came in handy. She quietly looked over her shoulder and said that I was lying *(xao)* and continued to walk away.

"Well, Joe, I gave it a shot," I said, almost relaxed that my feeble attempt was over.

A few minutes later she came back and stood next to me giving the girl bartender her orders. Joe kept elbowing me. Almost without thinking, I reached into my fatigue pocket for the necklace that I had bought for Mai. I placed the black velvet box on her tray and told her again in Vietnamese that I didn't lie and she was the most beautiful girl in all Vietnam. She walked away with the box on her tray, not acknowledging that it was even there, or making any other comments.

In a little while, she returned and politely, quietly, said thank you *(cảm ơn)*. She then shyly returned to work. I sat at the bar until it was almost emptied and Joe had left hours before. Then, as if in a dream, she appeared in front of me, across the bar. She asked if I could speak Vietnamese very well. I shook my head in the negative.

"*Dai Uy*, big BS-er!" she smiled.

"No, I'm not," I smiled back. "I really think you are a beautiful girl!"

We just looked at one another for what seemed forever. Something was happening… that certain something you can't explain. There was an immediate attraction and feeling for each other. We talked, we laughed. Two souls from different worlds had come together to share their lives. From that night on, we would be together almost every night for the next year. She was a part of my life now, and I a part of hers.

Her name was Lee. Lee was quite a story in her own right. When she was 17, she became pregnant by an American in Saigon. She left her home and her family to avoid any disgrace for them. She was raising her son on her own at Cam Ranh, keeping him a secret from her parents and sister. Her baby had just turned two years old.

We were from totally different cultures but we shared things that made us one. I was never closer to another human being than I was with Lee. She taught me the important things in life and severed my ties with the material world. Together we shared what life is all about. We accepted each other not for what was on the outside, but what was deep in our souls. Our story could fill another book, but I think it's important to know that Lee was a part of my story. Lee was a constant figure around the 764th and everybody was in love with her. She was the only girl in my life for a long time.

V.

The War Dogs and Their Handlers

THE 764TH WAS NOT only an outcast by personnel, but also by location. It was situated about five miles from nowhere in the middle of Cam Ranh Peninsula. I guess the top brass didn't want their sleep disturbed by barking dogs. It might lower property values. Just a few hundred yards away was the Air Force's main storage for POL (petroleum, oil and lubricants). Large, multi-thousand gallon tanks holding high octane jet fuel. This was a constant target for rocket attacks and nobody wanted this stuff in their neighborhood. I kind of liked being as far away from the real Army as possible.

My first official duty as the Commanding Officer of the 764th was to call a general staff meeting. Porter assembled everyone and called them to attention and they all saluted in unison. I returned the salute with my middle finger extended, smiling. They already knew what kind of guy I was from working around Holmgren.

"Now, all you major BS-ers sit down! That will be the last official Army crap this unit will do," I announced. "We are no longer covered by the Army Mickey Mouse rules unless we're putting on a show for some regular Army clowns. I expect you to give your best 24 hours a day to the dogs under our care. This place will be spotless, odorless and Army-less. I don't care what kind of Army record you've had in the past or how good or bad you think you are. Your record starts right now, with me!"

I shook each of their hands and from that day forward, a bond developed that was made stronger as time passed. We worked as a team, not as an officer giving orders to someone that took them because they had to. We had a common mission to save every dog that came to us and never give up.

The facilities at the 764th were the best the Army had to offer. The main hospital was built out of wood, painted green, with a steel roof. It was divided into two sections separated by a breezeway. On one side was the office area which contained a general office with several desks for the E.M.s. Then there was my office, a pharmacy and a bedroom. On the other side was the hospital area divided into a laboratory, an X-ray room, a storage room, a treatment room and surgery. This side was even air conditioned with two large York units. We also boasted the only flush toilet at Cam Ranh Bay. Because of the large water demand for the dogs, we also had a 10,000 gallon water tower which always provided enough water for the dogs, toilet and shower.

The Army spared no expense in equipping this unit. I had stuff the average vet could only dream about. The dogs and their value warranted any expense, as you will learn. In the back of the hospital were ten covered, concrete and steel kennels for the hospitalized cases. About 100 feet away, sharing the same compound, was the 981st M.P. Company that housed 120 sentry dogs. The 764th was the main entry point for dogs arriving in Vietnam. They were acclimated and further trained here. We were also responsible for all the dogs in the I and II Corps. These dogs were attached to combat units scattered from the DMZ (Demilitarized Zone) to Saigon in exotic places like Nha Trang, Phan Rang, Da Lat, Pleiku, Tuy Hoa, Da Nang, Phu Bai, Hue, Chu Lai, Qui Nhon, Bong Son and Buon Ma Thuot. I'm sure that just their very names bring back a host of feelings to anyone who has been in these hell-holes.

At the entrance to our compound was a seven-foot plywood cut-out of Snoopy with a doctor's bag in one paw with the words, "The Fightin' 764th". In the other paw was the green cross flag of the Veterinary Corps. The perimeter was dotted with sand bag bunkers and rows of concertina wire 6-9 feet high, completely surrounding the compound. As a kid, I once had a dream about being in a different world where the people and animals were strange; where the sights, sounds, language, and plants were unusual. Looking around, I knew that dream had become a reality!

The Army had three basic types of war dogs used in Vietnam. The most common of these was the sentry dog. All of them were German Shepherds. This breed was selected because of their great adaptability to all environments from the Arctic to the Tropics. The sentry dogs were used to patrol military installations and were under the constant, direct command of their handlers. They were on a leash at their handler's side unless they were on the attack. These dogs were trained at Lackland Air Force Base in the U.S. and shipped to Okinawa for their tropical training and adjustment to the high temperatures of 'Nam. They weighed over 80 pounds and it was all muscle. I'll never forget the first time I tried taking a blood sample from one of these steel critters. With five people holding tightly and bracing myself against the table, I pulled his leg forward to straighten it for the I.V. and he easily pulled my 210 pounds off the ground with his one leg!

Sentry dogs were trained using two different collars. One was the typical choke chain which was used in the instruction phase of training. While this was on, the sentry dog appeared fairly docile and looked to his handler for commands and instruction. The other was a two-inch leather collar that was used when the sentry dog was on patrol. As soon as this collar was placed around the dog's neck, there was a sudden transformation from Dr. Jekyll to Mr. Hyde… all teeth, fur and muscle… a killing machine!

When the 981st M.P. had a discipline problem among their ranks, the individual would be singled out and used in the training of these dogs and several options were open to them.

One way was to put the individual in a well-padded robot-like attack suit with a narrow slit for their eyes. A handler would agitate his dog in the direction of the attack suit and then release him. Even standing in a thick attack suit, the charge of the powerful sentry dog can be very intimidating. These dogs quickly found the weak points of this attack suit and went right for them. One point was at the neck where the helmet came to the shoulders and the other was in the groin area. If you protected your gonads, your throat would get ripped. These suits cost the Army over $300 apiece and lasted for about three attacks. This constant agitation was a daily part of training for a sentry dog. Before they went on patrol, they would all line up with their handlers and the man in the attack suit would run up and down in front of them.

Another M.P. discipline was to use a sentry dog with a bite-proof muzzle. These muzzles fit tightly over their face and teeth if applied properly, and prevented the dog from biting. They'd give some poor jerk about a 100-yard lead running and then let one of the sentry dogs after him. It was like watching a guided missile homing in on its target and hitting it in an explosion of sand, arms and legs. Even if the dog couldn't bite, he could still do a pretty good number on someone with his feet and body. These dogs were trained on movement and resistance. Your only defense was to cover your head and not move.

The minimum requirements for a sentry dog were to be at least 65 pounds and in perfect physical condition. They were mostly German Shepherds, but the Army accepted a lot of them that just looked like German Shepherds. We had one little female that only weighed 55 pounds and was the toughest little squirt I ever saw. One day it was time for her booster shot for one of her vaccinations. Dow was helping me and I told him to muzzle her.

"This little crapper ain't no trouble!" He boasted as he got her in a head-lock. "Go ahead and stick her, Doc."

As I entered the kennels, she slipped Dink's grip and had him cornered to the back of the run. I moved quickly out and closed the cage door. Dow stood motionless as she snarled in front of him.

"This little crapper is no trouble, huh?" I taunted. "Looks like you got your ass between a rock and a hard place."

Dow tried to move slowly along the side of the run to safety but she got closer and more threatening. He was just within arm's reach of the gate when she launched herself straight up at Dow's throat. If it wasn't for Dow's strength and size, he would have been hamburger. A little luck didn't hurt any. As she was in mid-air, Dink was able to grab at her neck and push her back enough to have a split second to make his exit. He looked at me and gave that silly laugh that only he could do. He never took any chances after that.

These were extremely well-trained dogs for attacking and I would put any one of them against any man alive... in fact, any two or three men. Before I actually saw one of these dogs in action, I was probably like a lot of people and compared them to other dogs I had been around. I figured that they couldn't be all that bad. I wrestled my 100 pound dog before and could overpower her. I've seen mean dogs before in practice, but you take an animal that is trained six hours a day and worked eight hours a night and fed like an athlete; you have a critter that's as hard as nails with teeth that can snap any bone in your body like a twig.

About 98% of these dogs were males, but females were accepted if they were spayed. In general, males are usually more aggressive. Shepherds were not only selected because of their environmental adaptability, but they were also the easiest breed to retrain to another handler. Most dog handlers' tours of duty lasted one year, but for the dogs, this was a one-way ticket until the war was over. If a handler returned stateside or if he was killed in action, it was necessary to be able to retrain his dog to a new man. This could be accomplished in two or three weeks.

While I was in New York, I was involved in the recruiting of dogs for the military. Out of 25 dogs examined, only two were taken. Because of the stringent physical and mental tests the Army required, very few were accepted. Hip dysplasia, a bone disorder in many large breeds, was the most common reason for rejection. Personality was another reason for rejection. Some were too fearful or shy, while others were plain crazy. Most of these dogs were donated by people who were just tired of them. A few had their papers and were even ex-show dogs.

The second category of war dogs was the trackers. Most of these were Labrador Retrievers and were used to track the enemy once they were spotted. They tracked very well until the VC learned to use this trait in setting up ambushes once they were tailed. Most of these dogs were like friendly house pets, but a few learned to survive by being vicious. Most of the trackers had already been phased out by the time I was in Vietnam. I only saw two.

The third type of dog was the off-lead scout dog. Now, this was a remarkable animal! Word had it that they were trained initially by a bunch of hippies at Fort Benning, Georgia. When a dog went into the military, he was classified at Lackland. The very aggressive became sentry dog candidates, while those that exhibited a high degree of intelligence became scout dogs. Unlike the sentry dogs, they were trained without discipline, using only rewards when they performed correctly.

Some of these dogs were almost super human, or at least most of them could perform superhuman feats. They could detect enemy ambushes up to 500 meters away. They could detect hidden tunnels and booby traps. Some were trained on contraband such as finding weapons, drugs, etc. Some were completely docile, while others were better attack dogs than the sentry. They would work "off-lead" in front of their handler at a distance of 100 yards or better. Some had radio control collars that could be used by their handlers for communication. Most, however, were controlled by silent hand signals given by their handlers. Thumbs down meant to lay down; thumbs up meant to get up; palm out forward meant to stay; closed fist directed downward from the wrist meant to crawl; moving the hand with the fingers extended, meant to go forward or move to the left or right. Also, each handler developed his own set of verbal commands that were a part of each team's personality.

Each scout dog had his own unique way of alerting the presence of danger. Some would point to it or its direction like a well-trained hunting dog pointing out quail; others would simply stop and refuse to move. Each handler became accustomed to what his dog was alerting. Most dogs alerted differently to different dangers. Booby traps dictated one course of action; an enemy ambushes another; a tunnel emplacement still another.

After a few combat units could actually see these dogs in action, there was a tremendous demand for them. They immediately became the most important piece of equipment in the unit. Every day they were on patrol meant the saving of human lives. They were turning out to be the best weapon against the VC and his guerrilla war that the Army ever developed. The Army always put a price tag on everything, and they estimated the value of a scout dog after training to be about $24,000. A small price tag when compared to a multi-million dollar missile – and a scout dog was a whole lot more useful. In the jungle, rice-paddy and mountain war that this turned out to be, conventional weapons were practically worthless. The VC was doing a pretty good job using rifles, booby traps, tunnels and, in some cases, bows and arrows.

Modern science and the military could not have designed a better weapon against the Viet Cong than this scout dog, which was the only thing better at this game than Charlie. The VC quickly recognized the value of this new weapon. They offered bounties to kill as many of these dogs and their handlers as possible. Each military dog was tattooed in his ear with the letter "M" and three numbers for identification. In order for a VC to collect his bounty, he had to cut off the tattooed ear for proof. This would be $1,500 cash; the handler's life was worth only $500. Many times in a fire fight, half the VC would be shooting at the scout dog, and our forces would be trying to make sure they didn't kill him or at least if the dog was killed, they wouldn't get his ears.

There were two different opinions in the Army upper brass concerning the use and the further development of scout dogs. On one side, you had the Army type who wants more men and more elaborate weapons, bigger and better and more costly. How could a 'dumb mutt' replace their expensive toys? On the other side, the guys in the front lines, the jungle rats who lived with war every day, thought these dogs were heaven-sent. A lot of these dogs were killed by booby traps and ambushes despite their training, but each dog's life meant the savings of dozens of human lives. The dogs that survived their tests of courage under the harsh circumstances of Vietnam for more than a couple of months were really special and respected.

The handlers of these war dogs were also as special and unique as their dogs. They became loners, but not by choice. Their main concern in life was the life of their dog. This isolated them from the mainstream of regular Army life. The only thing they were sure of was each other.

There was another big difference between sentry dog handlers and scout dog handlers. Because sentry dog handlers were closer to large Army and Air Force bases and were usually assigned to M.P. units, they were more Army proper. They usually had to pass a daily inspection by an M.P. sergeant. Their uniforms were pressed, caps starched and boots shined. Both their appearance and the appearance of their sentry dog had to be perfect. Their main patrols were at night, rarely during the day. After a night patrol, they both slept until noon and then there were afternoon training and preparation for night patrol.

Scout dogs, on the other hand, were mainly used on day patrols. These dogs and their handlers were assigned to units in the boonies where no one cared how shiny your boots were or if you had a bath that day. The scout dog handlers were a rag-tag bunch of outlaws who had little respect for anything except their own dog. Each dog was more than just part of the handler's life... it was his right arm. They ate the same food, slept together and shared a constant life of danger. They came as a matched set and no ties to anything or anyone except each other. These dogs didn't make friends with anyone too easily and maybe for good reason. They didn't need anyone except their own handler. No one else was to be trusted. Their lives depended on each other. The scout dog worked alone about 100 yards in front of his handler who in turn, worked a couple of hundred yards in front of an advancing patrol or company. This unique bond between man and animal will be more obvious as the story progresses.

The kennels in back of the 764th Hospital.

The dunk tank for all dogs arriving at the 764th. All new arrivals were de-ticked in the dunk tank.

VI.

Sherman the German and Tennis Shoes

I SETTLED IN QUICKLY as the C.O. of the 764th and started to finally feel my worth as a veterinarian. My entire job now was the care of Army dogs. I never felt much like a "Commanding Officer". There wasn't a big difference in the ages of my men and myself. Some of them were college graduates and a couple more years of college and they'd be in my position. Our relationship became more of friends working together for a common purpose. During the day, I'd let them wear whatever was comfortable... cut-offs, no shirts, sometimes bare-footed. I don't think anyone was ever in full uniform unless Major Kraft or Colonel Lamarr was headed our way.

We were always warned ahead of time that they were on the prowl by the clerk of the 176th. J.B. and other clerks at Cam Ranh had this tight grapevine and hung together. Major Kraft, like a good lifer, always followed SOP for officers and reported his every action and movement to the clerk before leaving the office. Communication by phone was excellent on the peninsula. Once the alarm was sounded that the brass was on the way, everyone did his best impersonation of an Army lifer... put on boots and tucked their long hair under their hats. Everyone would man their assigned "battle stations" and wait for the major's "surprise" appearance. J.B. would be typing some fictitious letter, Porter would be filing reports, Snake would be hanging over his microscope and Bell and Dow would be doing some phony treatment or procedure on "Sherman the German."

Sherman the German fit perfectly into this façade of an Army unit. How in the hell did this dog make it all the way to Vietnam? He had flunked out of every war dog school the Army had to offer. He failed sentry dog school because he wasn't aggressive enough. He flunked out of scout dog school because he wasn't smart enough. He flunked out of booby trap detection because he was too clumsy. And, he flunked contraband detection because he started to like the smell of marijuana.

Sherman and Snake would get along fine, but Sherman got along with everyone, including the Vietnamese. He was the only dog that Lee could play with and pet. He was everybody's "pet." Sherman would have washed out sooner if he wasn't such a good looking dog… black and tan, purebred AKC (American Kennel Club) registered German Shepherd. He could have won "Best of Show" in sentry dogs, if there were such a thing. All his training gave Sherman a great personality. He'd stand outside the obstacle course watching the other dogs bust their balls, and if a dog could laugh, he was doing it. He had trained himself not to play any of the Army's games… a flower child German Shepherd.

The only time I ever saw any aggression out of Sherman was when we were carrying an incapacitated dog on a stretcher past his run. He'd go nuts barking and attacking unless the other dog showed any signs of life. Then, he would cowardly lower his head and lay down. Sherman was allowed a free run of the entire compound like a house dog. When Major Kraft found out about Sherman, he notified the brass above me in Saigon that I had a worthless Army consumer. In a short time, I received orders from the top to terminate Sherman immediately. This was his death warrant. The Army didn't have any use for a "pet".

"You can't put Sherman away, Captain K," Dink pleaded.

"Right on!" agreed J.B. "He's the only dog in Vietnam that likes me."

I had no intention of seeing Sherman killed for any reason, but every dog that died or was euthanized for any reason had to have a post-mortem and tissue samples of all their internal organs sent to Saigon for complete analysis. They would expect Sherman's samples as part of my directive. However, as Sherman's luck would have it, the same day we had a DOA (dead on arrival) of another dog that was killed in a rocket attack. So, on this dog's post-mortem, I took two sets of samples… one for that dog, and one marked with Sherman's name and number.

There was no way for a pathologist to I.D. Sherman by his guts. Sherman was now officially dead and removed from the Army's records. Every time Major Kraft saw this dog we gave him a different name and condition he was being treated for. Kraft never recognized him as the same dog and Sherman maintained his prestigious position as the unofficial mascot of the 764th Medical Detachment.

One more quirk of fate added to this anti-Army unit. I never looked like your typical Army officer. As a matter of fact, I didn't look much like a veterinarian, or at least what people and Hollywood picture as a veterinarian. Taller and larger than average with long hair and a mustache, I looked like a borderline hippie. In vet school, they required a shirt and tie as a part of the dress code. So, I would wear a sweatshirt and a horrible green and purple polka-dot tie. I was always anti-establishment. I liked the idea of jungle fatigues; big, floppy and comfortable. You never had to make any big decisions of what to wear for the day or if the colors matched.

However, Army boots left a lot to be desired and they certainly didn't fit my style or feet. But luck or fate, or whatever mysterious forces are at action in the world, changed this situation.

As I said before, Cam Ranh Bay was a peninsula and on three sides were some of the best beaches in the world. If Hilton ever discovers them, it will be a condominium city. Whenever I had the time or was in the mood, I could stop my jeep, grab my snorkel and flippers and head for some of the best skin-diving anywhere. Except for nearly drowning with Holmgren, I never had a close call. Now that Ray was gone stateside, I did most of my diving alone – something no one should ever do, and looking back, I was very foolish. But, two things happened that ended my love of the ocean.

The best snorkeling was on a three mile stretch of beach separated into two areas… one called the Army Beach, the other the Air Force Beach.

I usually went to the Air Force Beach because it had better coral formations that weren't far off shore. This particular day, I was looking for something different. At the Army Beach, all the good diving was over a mile from shore in a bunch of small rock islands. I swam from island to island enjoying the solitude when all of a sudden I heard cries for help from just around a large rock in front of me. My first thought was that these two guys were just clowning, but when they caught sight of me, the calls became more frantic. I swam quickly to them and climbed onto the barren rocks.

"What's up?" I asked the desperate faces.

"Our friend went down with scuba gear and must have gotten into trouble. His tanks came up but we can't find him!" One frantically said.

These jerks were diving with no experience, using borrowed tanks in 40-50 feet of water that would have been tricky even for an experienced diver.

"How long has he been down?" I asked.

"Maybe ten to fifteen minutes!" One answered.

I figured if they thought ten-fifteen minutes, it might have been shorter because of their panic. As I was about to dive down, a body surfaced. One of the others and I dove into the choppy water and pulled the limp form up and onto the rocks. I had some basic CPR, but this would be the first time I ever used it on a human. The other two didn't have any training. I cleared his airway and started mouth to mouth resuscitation. It was difficult to fill his lungs with any air and when I began pushing on his chest, a large amount of salt water and fluid escaped from his lungs and stomach.

"DAMN, DAMN!" I gasped, pulling my face away from the fumes.

"How much did this guy have to drink?"

The smell of beer and booze was enough to knock you over.

"We were having a short-timer party for him. He's only got two weeks left in country."

I shook my head and continued CPR. *Two weeks left in country.* The words made me even more determined to save this guy. Two weeks left, after a whole year, and now he was probably dead. The more I tried, the worse he looked. He had this pale green appearance, no life, no pulse. I must have tried for another 15-20 minutes more before I gave up. I looked at the other two, who still had that look of horror on their faces. I shook my head. During the time that I was doing CPR, another person had arrived and by now was getting shore help.

"Maybe if we could get him to a hospital," one desperately said.

"It's all over now," I said quietly. "Let's get him into this life-ring and get him to shore. There's nothing else we can do. We're a long way from shore."

I jumped into the water to receive his body from the other two. The rocks were covered with coral and barnacles that had already cut me in several places. They lowered his skinny body down into the life-ring. I don't think the guy could have weighed more than 130 pounds. I pulled his arms through the ring and pulled him backwards. We started to shore, the three of us pulling the ring as we went. His face was over backwards, his eyes rolled back looking at me.

"I did my best," I started talking to him. "Two weeks left and you pull this shit!"

I kept thinking about his family back home. Maybe he had a

girlfriend or wife waiting. What about his mother, father, sisters or brothers? Now, everything was over because of a stupid mistake. Now, instead of a joyful reunion, it would be a tearful goodbye. I then turned my frustrations on the other two, who were looking at me like I had lost it.

"You dumb asses! You stupid _____ _____!" I wanted to yell at them as they stared, dumbfounded.

I wanted to start pounding on them, but one look at their faces and their eyes and I knew they would pay for this the rest of their lives. The memory would be etched in their brains like this guy's face and eyes were burned in mine.

"Can you take him the rest of the way yourself? We can't go any farther!" One said.

I looked at both of them in disbelief. Maybe they were tired. Maybe the booze and the reality of the situation caught up with them. Or maybe they thought I had lost my mind. I waved goodbye to them as they swam to the nearest island. When I finally touched the safety of the sand bottom, I was exhausted. I kept thinking *why isn't anyone coming out to help?* Finally, some people came out to meet me and pulled the body the rest of the way to a waiting ambulance. I didn't say my goodbyes as they loaded him into the back of the ambulance. I walked up the beach to my jeep and left.

I confined my swimming to the Air Force Beach from that day. I couldn't get the memory of that guy's face erased from my mind. I should have stopped all beach action. It never dawned on me that we faced danger from sharks, towing a body while bleeding from coral cuts. This was pre-*Jaws* era and I never gave them a second thought.

On one occasion, I did see a shark. It was during the monsoon season and the high surf caused a lot of fish to be killed on the coral reef. When I saw a large shark feeding around my route, I figured it was time to head for shore. I had already cleared the reef and was walking in waist deep water on a perfectly clear sand bottom. All of a sudden, I stuck my toes into something that looked like red moss floating just off the bottom. It was like putting my foot into the molten steel of Number Three Open-Hearth furnace at Inland Steel. By the time I reached the shore, the pain was unbearable! I tried rubbing the area with sand. I tried massaging it. Everything I did made it worse.

On the way back to the BOQ, I stopped at an Army clinic. The young doctor shrugged his shoulders and told me to try Benadryl. After a sleepless night, I headed for the specialists at the Air Force Hospital. My leg had swollen up to my groin and I didn't want it to go any further: at least not without a love interest.

"I feel sorry for you, captain," the sergeant said at the front desk.

"We've got six more just like you in the hospital and we don't have any answers."

I thought at first he was trying to bullshit me or just scare me.

"Listen, sergeant. I'm a veterinarian. I've had as much or more training than some of the doctors around here. Just give me what they're treating the rest with and I'm history," I said confidently.

"You get off that leg right away or you'll be history alright!" another voice answered.

A young Air Force doctor convinced me that the sergeant wasn't BS-ing. Some of the others had already lost fingers and toes. We were all victims of some kind of sea creature that caused tissues to swell and then begin to rot. They pushed me to Ward 7 in a wheel chair. The only encouragement I got was that a panel of marine medicine specialists was called in from all over the Far East and would be examining all of us the next morning. I'll be out of here in no time!

The next morning all seven of us victims were lined up in wheel chairs. I was the only one affected in the left foot. All the rest were on the right foot and leg. One guy had been there for months. Some had toes missing and rotting. I was the only one among them with any medical experience and I sat there in disbelief listening to these so-called experts from Hawaii, Japan, Australia and the Philippines discussing each of our conditions.

"The ischemia and necrosis are dramatic in all these cases!" One announced. "Edema is universal with little erythema."

The medical jargon was flowing like they were speaking in a foreign tongue, as not to alarm us. The bottom line translation was they didn't have any idea in hell what was wrong with us or how to treat this crap. We had a bad case of incurable "crud". They questioned each of us as to what we saw. After about an hour with these Einsteins, they decided to use a different course of treatment on every one of us. We were all pushed back to Ward 7. I had never been in a hospital since I had my tonsils out when I was five. The guy on my right was suffering from warts on his ass. I mean, seriously, you can't make this stuff up. He had warts on his rear and went to the area Army clinic. The doctor there was above doing ass warts so he had his assistant Spec. 5 do it. The process then required a liquid cautery solution to be applied after a local anesthetic. Well, the Spec. 5 got a little sloppy or hurried and the solution ran down this guy's crack and all over his testicles, causing third degree burns!

"How can I write home and tell them I'm in the hospital because they burned my balls trying to remove ass warts?" Wart pleaded (the only name we ever called him was "Wart").

"And you know what's really bad? What's really fucking bad? They didn't get rid of the damn warts and I've got to get them burned all over again… and today is the day!"

Wart kept everyone laughing. You only had to look in his direction and crack up. The only way this guy could sleep was to prop up his back with pillows, with his feet flat on the mattress, or, sleep face down with his ass straight up in the breeze.

Most of the others in this ward of ten weren't as funny as Wart. Across from me was another guy who got fed up with the war after receiving a *Dear John* letter and tried to get sent home early by shooting himself in the leg. The first thing you should consider when trying to wound yourself is the caliber of the weapon you're using. You don't slightly hurt yourself with a .45 caliber pistol unless your aim is very accurate. They took his leg off from the knee down. He was scheduled to be transferred to the infamous "Ward 8" for mental rehabilitation. There really was a "Ward 8" just for people who went over the edge.

Then, there was another poor sucker with some kind of ulcerations on his lungs. If this guy wasn't sent home, then nobody was leaving this country alive. Every morning and evening, two nurses would come in and lay him over the edge of his bed until his head was almost on the floor and then commence to slap and beat on his back until he coughed up all kinds of blood tinged fluids and clots. Anyone for dessert?

Then there was the collection of seven ocean-life tragedies like myself. Every one of them had a different horror story about some mythical sea creature that attacked them.

"It was this hideous sea creature, like in a bad dream!" one related.

"It attacked me so fast, I could barely see it. It was like a bolt of lightning!" said another.

A couple more days of this crap and I would be hallucinating, talking to the walls and ready for Ward 8!

"Come on, doctor! I know more about this crap than you do," I said one morning, "And I certainly know what the hell it was… just some floating moss. We're a bunch of fuckin' guinea pigs. This guy is on antihistamines, this one on antibiotics and I'm the steroid freak! If you're not signing me out, then I'm taking a hike!"

"OK, Dr. Kubisz, if the swelling stays down another day, I'll sign you out," the doctor relented.

"But you're on your own. I'm not taking any responsibility."

"Don't let him go, Doc, don't let him go! He's in agony. Let him suffer in here with the rest of us!" Wart yelled.

"Yeah, right, Doc! Don't let him go, don't let him go, don't let him go!" they all chanted.

What the doctor didn't know was the reason for this sudden popularity wasn't my magnetic personality. Every night after lights out, my men would sneak into the ward with a couple of bottles of booze and we party half the night. Every morning the nurses thought we were all a bunch of diabetics because of the high glucose in our urine specimens. Also, I couldn't let it be known that I was incapacitated for a minute. If Kraft found out I was hospitalized, I could say goodbye 764th. It was already a week and I kept in close contact with the unit every day. Bell learned to forge my signature.

"Any chance of being sent home right away?" I asked the next morning after sleeping all night with my foot elevated to keep it from swelling.

"No way! The only way anyone goes home early is in a black bag. We have to get our experience somewhere before charging our high prices stateside," the doctor laughed. "I'll write something up and have the colonel sign it."

The doctor must have seen the writing on the wall and wrote a beautiful, official letter for me to carry around:

To Whom It May Concern:
Captain John B. Kubisz, VC, has suffered a war-related injury that has required extensive treatment and hospitalization. He has the opportunity to be shipped stateside, but has declined and will finish his work as the C.O. of the 764th Medical Detachment. However, he must wear tennis shoes because of recurrent

swelling of his feet that may last indefinitely. For any other information on his condition, please contact me at the Air Force Hospital, Cam Ranh Bay. Captain Kubisz is a credit to our efforts in South Vietnam.

Colonel Marshal W. Cohen, MD

I was practically a hero. Who's going to challenge this official BS? A letter from a full-bird colonel, updated, follow-up left open, was too good to be true. Wait till the major sees me boppin' around in tennis shoes!

The bad news was that this foot problem persisted. Day after day, my toes, feet and lower leg would swell if I was on my feet for more than an hour. Some of my toes became rotten and the flesh fell off, leaving large holes. If I elevated my foot and drank plenty of bourbon, it got better. The consensus of the marine medical experts was that this was a new species of Fire Coral only identified in the South China Sea. They had no idea how to treat it. This news, coupled with the news of still another amputation of one of the others, left me in the pits. Booze and Lee helped me through the rough spots.

When I stopped feeling sorry for myself, I realized that if I was going to get better, the cure rested in my hands. What would I do if I were an animal presented to me for treatment? I'd have to do a little experimenting. Horses often have trouble with their legs swelling. Their treatment involved wrapping their legs with elastic bandages and physical therapy. So, I started wrapping my legs from my toes to my hip. I stopped drinking entirely and started physical therapy and massage. When I felt better, I started running and lifting weights. I lost 30 pounds and was lean and mean. I made a complete recovery within a month, but my tennis shoes remained forever a part of my life.

VII.

The Cases

THE 764TH MEDICAL DETACHMENT was a little different from the average vet hospital in the States. For one thing, all my patients were over 50 pounds and none of them were anxious to see me. But, a lot of the problems were similar to cases back home. Every morning was a sick call for the 981st dogs and I could always count on at least a half a dozen dogs and their handlers waiting in the breezeway. There was always the usual collection of assorted cuts, eye problems and skin problems. The heat was as difficult for the dogs as it was for the people; heat exhaustion and heat stroke were common. Gastric torsion, a condition seen in large breeds where the stomach becomes twisted, was also common and usually fatal.

All the dogs required basic maintenance like a well-tuned sports car. Every dog was kept up-to-date on vaccinations, and with some vaccines, this meant every two months. Leptospirosis, a common kidney disease in Vietnam, required boosters every two months to be effective. Even giving a simple vaccination was an experience. I remember one incident in the breezeway.

A sentry dog named "Killer" was due for his lepto booster. Normally, I had someone with experience holding dogs help me. But, since Dink and Bell were in the office and Killer had a bite-proof muzzle on, I thought it would be safe. I had the handler lock his arm around Killer's neck and I sat on my haunches in the back of Killer. I pulled his skin up and quickly made the injection. In a flash, Killer was loose and turned towards me, knocking me flat on my ass and back. I grabbed him by the throat as he trashed me with his feet, his breath right in my face. The handler wasn't able to pull his dog off me until Dow and Bell came from the office area and helped out. Both of them found it quite amusing... the C.O. getting his ass mauled by a dog.

"Haven't you ever had a 'dog' on top of you, Doctor K?" taunted Ding Dong.

"I'm only used to beauty queens!" I stabbed back, trying to get some composure back to my scratched body.

This incident only increased my respect for these animals. Monthly blood tests were a challenge. We needed to check for heartworm and do a CBC (complete blood count). Stool samples were checked for a variety of internal parasites. I think every disease and parasite in the world was common in 'Nam. The external parasite that plagued us the most was the common dog tick. At Cam Ranh, the dogs were bathed and dipped monthly, but in some of the out-of-the-way camps, ticks were bad enough to produce anemia from their blood sucking.

I once saw a dog in Phan Rang that was so anemic he required a blood transfusion. The inside of his ear looked like a dried sunflower, but with ticks instead of seeds. Within a radius of seventy miles of Cam Ranh Bay, there was every type of topography you could imagine... the rolling hills, brush and sand of Cam Ranh; the coastal plains almost devoid of trees; the endless rice fields to the south; the thick jungles to the north and the almost mountainous highlands of the interior. Most of the time, I had to go where the dogs were assigned to do their monthly physicals. The terrain and climate of some of these places would really surprise many people when they think of Vietnam. I know they surprised me. I had the misconception that everywhere in Vietnam had the 110 degree heat of Cam Ranh Bay.

One of my monthly trips was to a detachment of five dogs at Da Lat. They were up on Lang Bien Mountain, which was the second highest point in Vietnam at 6,700 feet. It was probably the prettiest spot in all of Vietnam, but I was not prepared for temperatures in the 50s in the day and 30s at night. It was the only spot in South Vietnam to ever report snow. My first trip to Da Lat started with 120 degrees at Cam Ranh and in a Huey helicopter. The only seat left was the side-gunner position. You must never show fear or look too green to the helicopter pilot or he'll make it worse for you. There I was, 210 pounds of a veterinarian, shaking and dangling by a thread of a seat belt over the side of a Huey!

"How high are we?" I yelled, trying to act like I gave a damn.

"About 5,000 feet," someone yelled. "We fly high to avoid the ground-fire!"

Reassuring, I thought. That's why I'm so cold and shaking like a leaf. I'll be warm when we land. It's not that far to Da Lat. What I didn't know was that from Cam Ranh, Da Lat was straight up. After landing and still shaking uncontrollably, I scrounged up a sweatshirt and a field jacket. We drove from the air strip in a three-quarter ton truck and up to Lang Bien Mountain. VC activity was increasing in the area and we kept alert for land mines and ambushes. I was really surprised at the condition of the five dogs on the mountain. They weighed more than the average, with beautiful, thick coats like they'd spent the winter in Hayward, Wisconsin.

I only made one trip to Da Lat, because shortly after, Charlie overran the position and the dogs had to be immediately evacuated to Cam Ranh. Dogs that were used to 40 degrees now had to withstand 120. I ordered complete rest, plenty of cold water and a cold shower twice a day. Within two weeks, the dogs threw their coats and lost some weight. After a month, they were working in the tropical heat.

Some of the cases that I saw at Cam Ranh, I will never see again... they were so unusual. On sick call one morning, a handler presented me his sentry dog that had been bitten in the testicles the night before by a Bamboo Viper... a small foot-long, green snake with red eyes, that was quite poisonous (or as Snake would correct me, "venomous," when he identified the small snake that the handler managed to capture). Snake quickly picked up the viper with his bare hands and ran off with it like a kid with a new toy.

The snake's bite had already caused the scrotum to swell to the size of a volley ball. There was no other course of treatment except radical castration and total removal of the scrotum. I worried about making this attack dog into some kind of marshmallow, but to my surprise, the opposite happened. This dog was never anything special... slightly underweight and too nervous to train. But, within a month following his neutering, he gained 20 pounds and his entire attitude changed for the better. He wasn't any less aggressive but became one of the best dogs at the 981st M.P.s. When the other handlers saw the results, I was plagued by a rash of requests to neuter everybody's dog.

"I think old Ralph is having trouble with his rocks, Doc!" was the usual line. "You'd better cut them off!"

Neutering wasn't a bad idea for most of these dogs. Testicle problems were always a bother to these dogs because they were housed on concrete and suffered constant trauma from insects and brush. I initiated a neutering program and castrated as many as I could.

Because dogs were scattered all over I and II Corps, it was sometimes difficult to give them quick medical attention. If a sentry dog had a minor injury or illness, the local food inspector veterinarian would jump at a chance to treat a live animal. I didn't blame them; I would have done the same in their position. However, they may have had the talent and desire, but they greatly lacked the facilities and treatment options open to me.

Sometimes they would wait too long and by the time I saw them, it was too late. One of these cases was a dog named "Prince." Prince, according to his records, had a normal body weight of 85 pounds. By the time I saw him; he weighed 37 pounds and looked like a dehydrated Greyhound. He had to be carried into the hospital on a stretcher. One look at this beautiful sentry dog reduced to a pathetic mess and I vowed that this shit would never happen again. Heads were going to roll and I would never again see any delays in dogs being shipped to me. If they missed their morning breakfast, they would be shipped to me immediately or I would have someone's gonads on the chopping block! Major Kraft arrived on the scene shortly after Prince was admitted. He had this uncanny knack of showing up when he wasn't wanted. But, I think even he felt some remorse for this poor animal that was once a proud sentry dog. When I told him that I thought this dog had a chance, his old demeanor came forward.

"This sucker is already dead meat and doesn't know it. You're wasting the Army's time and money!" he sarcastically stated. "The colonel has to see this before you put it down." He made a hasty exit and got into his jeep.

A couple hours later, Colonel Lamarr arrived, minus Major Kraft.

"This is the worst case of neglect I've ever seen, John." The colonel said, hands on his hips, his paunch protruding under his fatigues. "I have to agree with the major this time. This dog doesn't stand a chance," he continued belching. "You'd better put him out of his misery."

"Colonel, I'm not here to put dogs away. I know it costs the Army money, but we don't learn anything if we don't at least try," I pleaded.

"Well," the colonel hesitated, "If this dog lasts another day, I'll be surprised anyway. So, go on ahead and give it a go. I'll try to calm the major down. Boy, he's becoming a real pain in the ass!"

Prince had lost any aggression he possessed and was reduced to something barely above death. We were all determined that this dog would not die. I ordered every blood test known and the cultures of the blood and urine. The results led us to the diagnosis of an acute kidney infection that was resistant to every antibiotic known to me. Unlike the Vietnamese water buffaloes, our dogs quickly became immune to common antibiotics like penicillin and if they were in Vietnam for any time, they became resistant to most of them. Prince's culture revealed a bacterial infection that only an antibiotic called "Keflex" would kill.

"What the hell is a Keflex?" I asked. "I'll call the Air Force Hospital and see if they know."

Keflex, I found out, was a fairly new antibiotic at that time, almost experimental and very difficult to get. I told some supply sergeant the situation and that I needed about two grams a day for ten days to two weeks of treatment.

"What do you guys have to offer for a couple of boxes of Keflex? We don't just give this shit away!" the sergeant boldly stated.

I really couldn't think of anything we had that a big hospital wouldn't have. Then it dawned on me that we sometimes received some of the Air Force Hospital shipments by mistake. Just a couple days before, a shipment of six dermatome cables arrived and we didn't even know what they were used for. I'll offer them to this jerk.

"Could you use a couple of dermatome cables?" I asked.

"New ones?" was the reply.

"Brand new!" I said. "But, you'd better make it worth my while!" I said with determination, sensing the eagerness in his voice.

"You can have all the Keflex you want for a couple of them babies," the sergeant replied.

I took the six cables and headed for the Air Force Hospital. I was determined to get as much as I could in trade. One look at the six dermatome cables and they were willing to trade half of their hospital. I got a few boxes of Keflex, a bunch of surgical drapes, an assortment of surgical instruments, 20 sheets of three-quarter inch plywood (4 x 8 feet) and a case of T-bone steaks.

As soon as I returned to the 764th, we started Prince on a gram of Keflex I.V. every twelve hours and waited. We had already started supportive care with lactated ringer's solution I.V. According to his chart, Prince had not eaten any solid food for 30 days! The big trade and the case of steaks were all it took to call for an immediate celebration. It wasn't unusual to party after-hours at the 764th. We were out of the way and no one ever bothered us after dark. J.B. provided the sounds, beverages of your choice were always available and the port vet or myself could always find the food. Even after I left the port, I would show up dock-side and check the ship's manifest. If I saw something, I took it. If I was stopped by the M.P.s, I would present them with my clipboard and have them sign it. Once I was stopped with a case of lobster (40 pounds).

"Halt, captain, sir!" an M.P. announced. "I must see your authorization for that case of lobster and your reason for this pilferage, sir!"

"No pilferage, private," I returned. "This is serious business. I'm taking this for samples. There's been an outbreak of hepatitis and we think it's in the lobster. We've already had some colonel damn near die. Now, sign this requisition before I put your ass on the report!"

"Hepatitis! You don't know what in the hell to eat anymore!" the M.P. answered, as he signed anything I had on the clipboard.

The dermatome cables were used at the Air Force Hospital in skin grafts. Most veterinarians have never done a skin graft, let alone use a dermatome. But, anyway, it was time to relax, have a barbecue and down a few beers. By the afternoon, Prince received another gram of Keflex and by evening, the party was going strong. I stood in front of Prince's run in the back of the hospital. As I gnawed on the bone from the steak, I noticed that Prince started to sniff in my direction. This was the first sign of any life in him.

"Throw another steak on the 'cue for Prince," I ordered.
While the steak was cooking, Prince slowly lifted his head, then his whole body then stood up and slowly walked towards me. He put his nose up to the wire and I stuck the bone through the wire mesh. At first, he licked it slowly and tried to pull it through the bars. He downed one steak, then another, then a few potatoes and a half a loaf of bread! Everyone kept cheering him on! This again was against any principles of veterinary nursing care for an animal that hadn't eaten for 30 days, but it was such a thrill just to see him eat!

"We'd better stop for today, men. He's going to explode. I don't want him breaking down with diarrhea tomorrow," I said.

But tomorrow came and nothing unfavorable happened. We started him off with his Keflex injection, which now he resented and started him back on his regular sentry dog diet. I've never seen a dog ever eat like that before. We'd fill a giant bowl about the size of a cat litter box and he would eat it all...

four times a day. He was never full. In fourteen days, he had gained 21 pounds and looked great. I'm sure that the colonel and the major were so convinced that Prince had bought the farm, they never asked about him for three weeks. Then, one day on their monthly snoop-trip, they remembered him.

"Whatever happened to that poor, skinny dog you got in here about three weeks ago?" the colonel inquired.

"You're looking at him, sir!" I beamed

I thought both of them were going to drop their teeth as their eyes popped. The major grabbed the record chart from the front of the kennel and paged through it. Prince was now close to seventy pounds. I opened the run and got in with Prince and gave him a hug. We were old buddies by now. "Sure, captain," the major sneered, "You saved his life and now he's some kind of a pussy-pet... like that Sherman dog was!"

I wasn't sure what Prince was capable of doing as a sentry dog because since we had him, all he ever received was TLC, but I'd been around these dogs long enough to know that if Prince had anything left, I would get it out of him. Prince was already looking at these two jerks like he knew they pronounced his death verdict three weeks prior. Dogs can do those things, whether people believe it or not.

"Prince!" I yelled.

Prince responded and came to immediate attention, waiting my next command. I thought we'll show this clown some "pussy" sentry dog! I pointed in the direction of the major.

"ATTACK!!" I screamed.

It's a damn good thing the door to the run was between Prince and the major and only slightly opened. Prince lunged forward and hit the door shut like a steel trap, causing the major to almost fall backwards.

"You'd better watch your shit, captain!" Kraft managed to say, visibly shaken.

"You've proven your point, John," the colonel replied, somewhat shaken up himself.

Prince accomplished more than just returning to duty. He made it possible for all future dogs that were sick or injured to be shipped immediately to the 764th without any delays. I had written enough letters and filled out a dozen reports and made a few phone calls. I was successful in shaking up the troops. The general himself in Saigon issued some heavy duty orders that all dogs would be sent to me for any reason. No one else was allowed to treat them in the future. They would be medevacked by chopper as soon as possible, with no exceptions.

One of the other benefits Prince initiated was our indoctrination into the world of bartering and scrounging. If we needed something, it was almost impossible to get it through regular Army channels, or it took forever to get. The whole unit became very good at this game except for Granny, who always did things by the book. But, at least he kept his mouth shut and shared in the benefits. We even went one step further... stealing!

We never stole anything that was needed for the war effort, but if we could lay our hands on something slated to "pretty-up" some general's hooch, it was fair game. The entire 764th became a show-piece for the fine art of the black market. Our floors were tiled with green asphalt tile; we got a new refrigerator; we paneled the office area with three-quarter inch plywood and stained it a deep, dark oak. We didn't give a damn about the way we looked or how we dressed, but this hospital was home and it looked great! Everyone wanted to see it.

Just about every couple of weeks, some groups of dignitaries from the States (generals, congressmen, senators and reporters) would be shown our facilities and the sentry dogs would be put through their paces in the obstacle course and in their attack training. We would really lay on the BS as thick as possible. The end result of all this show was that there was more icing on the cake that we enjoyed with the general in Saigon. We were written up in the *Stars and Stripes* military paper and many other papers back home in the States.

As our successes continued, so did the closeness of the men in the unit. We were like brothers and a pretty good team. Granny didn't seem to fit in but provided the flux we needed to keep everything together, from an Army point of view. None of us ever gave up on the chase without a good fight, even when things looked hopeless.

We had one of these cases medevacked to us that received three wounds from an AK-47 (the Soviet's version of our M-16). One bullet shattered a rib and then broke up in the chest; the second went clean through the abdomen; the third shattered the femur (the large upper bone in the rear leg). Radiographs revealed that there wasn't enough bone left in the leg to repair the damage. However, the rib that was shattered could be removed and used for a bone graft to shore up the femur. This dog lost considerable blood and suffered from shock, so it was essential that we built him up before any surgery was attempted.

After he was stabilized, we started about 8AM (or for the lifers – 0800). We resected the rib and cleaned up the chest cavity. One bullet fragment had almost ripped through the aorta, which would have meant instant death. After six hours, the surgery on the thorax was completed and we proceeded to the abdomen. At this point, we took a break and ate lunch while we got additional blood into our patients.

The surgery on the abdominal area went beautifully and was uneventful, but time consuming. The entire length of the intestines had to be examined carefully for any perforations. It was surprising how little damage had occurred here. After another four hours, this part was finished and we prepared the section of removed rib to use it in the hind leg.

I applied the scalpel directly over the bullet-hole entrance in the leg and made a long eight-inch incision over the fracture site. One look at the tissues beneath my incision and I knew it was all over.

The high velocity bullet had done what it was developed to do. It was like a miniature bomb had exploded under the skin. All the tissues looked like so much garbage... no movement, no blood supply, no life! I always wondered why, with all the modern medicine at our disposal, someone had to lose an arm or leg. But after seeing first-hand the effects of man's ultimate weapons, there was no doubt in my mind that this leg was totally destroyed. I might have been able to save this dog's life if he was a pet in the U.S., but it meant complete amputation of the rear leg. Three-legged dogs can still make a very good pet. The Army, however, didn't have any use for a sentry dog that wasn't in peak condition.

I looked at the men around me. Ding, across the table from me, looked like hell after being up for thirty-six hours; he knew our efforts were down the toilet. Snake stood quietly shaking his head. Granny left the room probably to get the post-mortem jars and specimen jars. Bell, the unit's number one cheerleader, refused to accept the verdict.

"Come on, Doc!" Ding pleaded. "We can save him. Let's try something... anything!"

I shook my head in the negative and reluctantly administered the solution that would put this dog to sleep forever. It appeared that our ten-hour surgery marathon (the longest operation I've ever performed, before or since) was a losing battle. However, the effort coalesced us into a fine surgery team. We had conquered in one operation, all the difficulties encountered and even the complexities found in thoracic surgery. Losing any dog was a "bummer," as J.B. used to say. But one thing that we learned was never to give up on any case, no matter how bad it looked or how hopeless. Every case became a lesson, a training ground in trauma and emergencies.

The worst looking case was a dog named "Diablo." He was a large, almost black German Shepherd that had stepped on a trip-wire and had a hand grenade explode directly under him. At admission, he was standing with a hole as wide as the dog and from his head to his front legs. Even more amazing, was that the huge jugular veins and carotid arteries were not severed; there were no broken bones or loss of vision. However, both ear drums were destroyed and there was some blood in the ear canals. This dog appeared so hopeless that we kept him out of view and hidden at the 981st M.P.s. I didn't want another confrontation with the major or colonel.

Within three weeks the progress was phenomenal. Although the wound was too large to suture and a lot of tissue was completely blown away, I couldn't do anything except treat it as an open wound... cleaning it daily and using large doses of antibiotics. It had closed quickly to a third of its original size. The ear drums, however, did not show any regeneration. We learned from the other handlers that Diablo was the best dog they'd ever seen at detecting booby traps and couldn't understand why he screwed up. But, to make a long story short, Diablo was eventually shipped back to Okinawa and used to train other dogs in booby trap detection. It had been a theory for a long time that these dogs detected trip-wires by hearing the wind blowing over them like a string on an instrument. But this theory went right out the window with this dog... Diablo was totally deaf!

It was uncommon for a handler to get killed and not his dog, or vice-versa. They were a team matched for at least a year and the loss of one meant acute grief and depression for the other. When they separated at the end of the handler's tour of duty, both went through a similar state of depression. Sometimes both the handler and his dog were killed together. I remember one case that brought the war painfully close. Like I said before, most of the dogs, if possible, had a complete physical every month. On one of these routine check-ups, a handler on his way to a hot area presented me with his dog for examination. He was obviously proud of his dog and rightfully so. The dog was in fantastic shape… 110 pounds of muscle that made the handler look feeble in comparison. The handler looked like a skeleton.

"This is one of the best looking dogs I've seen in the Army!" I announced to his beaming handler.

"But, you are one of the skinniest dudes I've ever seen. Get on this scale and let's see what you weigh."

He stood on the scale, his jungle fatigues drowning him.

"Six foot, one inch, 128 pounds… uniform, boots and all," I announced. "You'd better stop giving your rations to your dog and start eating them yourself or your dog's going to out-weigh you," I laughed.

That night this handler and his dog took a direct hit from a rocket. Both were killed in an instant. By now, I was already into my six month extension. Why anyone would choose to stay in Vietnam for more than a year was a mystery to most guys who went there. Some of the guys that extended were in combat situations. I think a lot of them had already gone over the edge. You could see it in their eyes. They would not be able to function outside of 'Nam. But, there were a few like me who found their niche. I know that I changed, but I think for the better. When I asked Snake why he was on his second extension, he told me that he couldn't cope with the real world. The "real world" was a common expression everyone used in 'Nam.

When you were in Vietnam, all you thought about was going home. When you were in the States, all you thought about was 'Nam. But as much as you wanted to go home, the more you isolated yourself here. I did. And the longer you stayed, the harder it was to go back to the real world. By now, Lee was a big part of my life. Every day we shared a relationship that I would never be able to duplicate.

The only regret I had was keeping up with all the Army bullshit. Other than that, I had set up my own little world and I had everything I needed for my survival and happiness. The 764th was my unit, my first position of authority and responsibility. With the Dirty Half Dozen, we were isolated to fight our own battles, make our own mistakes, and revel in our successes. We were sort of a canine *M.A.S.H.* unit and I was Hawkeye Pierce.

I was no longer sleeping in the crowded BOQ. I slept at the 764th in the CQ (Charge of Quarters). At night, everything got very quiet, including the dogs. I shared the tropical nights with Lee. Our closest human neighbor was Spec. 5 Taylor of the 981st M.P.s who preferred night duty and was in charge of the compound while everybody slept. The rest of the personnel stayed at the main Army quarters five miles away. Taylor would monitor the radio and telephone calls and would notify me of any incoming wounded. One night he burst into the CQ without any warning. Let's say I was in a romantic mood with Lee.

"Captain, captain!!" he yelled as he flung the door open. "Rockets are coming in just over the ridge that separates us from the POL!"

I knew it was almost impossible for a rocket to get over the high ridge. They had tried before Taylor was assigned to his unit.

"Damn it, Taylor! You're enough to screw up a wet dream!" I yelled back at him. "What in the hell do you want me to do?"

"SOP dictates that we head for the bunkers!" he anxiously replied.

"What are you doing? Taking lessons from Granny? We have two choices. One, we can go to the dirty bunkers and get eaten by Snake's pets or we can stay in our rooms. Either way, if a rocket hits that jet fuel, we are all French fries! Now, get the hell out of here unless there's a real emergency because if I'm going to die, I'm going out doing this!!"

The VC was stepping up their activities again all over South Vietnam and Cambodia. Even protected Cam Ranh wasn't immune. A group of Viet Cong invaded the peninsula just a few miles away, blew up a bunch of stuff, inflicted a few casualties and escaped without anyone even firing a shot at them. All activities were ordered to tighten their security. We were told to expect more wounded than normal. Also, the POL and the dogs might be the next target for sabotage or snipers.

VIII.

Paper is Delivered

ONE NIGHT, I AWOKE SUDDENLY at 2:30 in the morning. Something had just crawled over my chest and my heart was pounding like a drum. You never get quite used to critters using you for their racetrack. I lay there staring at the ceiling in the darkness. I was wide awake. There were nights like this for everyone in Vietnam; when you were alone with your thoughts and if you ever stopped to think, your mind became your worst enemy. But, somehow, this night was different. I had developed this sense of premonition while I was in Vietnam and I wasn't taking any of Snake's weed. I knew when my critically ill aunt died before they notified me. I knew when my pet dog "Tinka" died before the letter arrived. And now, something else had happened or was going to happen and I was uneasy. I didn't have to wait long for my answer.

I could hear "Twinkle-Toes" Taylor's feet coming down the path from the 981st M.P. to the 764th. He walked quickly but not in a panic. He opened the side door and walked quietly to the CQ room.

"Captain?" he whispered. "I hate to disturb you, but I've just been radioed that a scout dog is coming in by chopper," he continued just outside my door.

"That's OK, Taylor. I'm already up. Something just crawled off me. I think it was one of Snake's pets. I want you to get the rest of the men, all of them, and have them report for duty," I ordered.

"All of them, even J.B.?" he asked, a bit surprised.

"I said... get their asses, including J.B.'s down here right away!" my voice somewhat louder.

I wasn't quite sure what this feeling was. First, I thought the upper brass was conducting some kind of test. They were good at that kind of crap.

I think they got their jollies off getting everyone up in the middle of the night just to watch them stagger around. Anyway, I wasn't taking any chances. If this was some kind of a test Major Kraft was pulling, then we were going to pass with flying colors. I got dressed, got the hospital lights on and got the equipment ready. In a few minutes, everybody was there, rubbing their eyes, half-dressed and complaining.

"What the hell is going on, Dr. K?" Bell asked.

"Yeah! What the H-E-L-L is happening? I'm a clerk: clerks work nine to five!" J.B. responded.

"I knew some kind of shit was going to happen tonight, I just knew it," replied Dink.

"Either we have some kind of screwed up Army drill, or we have a real scout dog coming in. Either way, we are going to be prepared. I just find it awfully funny that we have a scout dog being medevacked in the middle of the night," I said.

You could already make out the unmistakable sound of a helicopter in the distance. As we stood in the hospital breezeway, the night sky was lit up by a million stars in the unpolluted sky. The sounds of the chopper's blades intensified, and the landing beacons of the Huey pierced the darkness. It came down and landed gently on the landing pad outside the entrance to the compound. Ding Dong and Dinky waited with a stretcher.

"Let's get 'em!" I yelled and ran with Ding and Dink to the chopper's side doors.

A tall, slim, blond-haired G.I. jumped out first. I could make out the insignia of the 101st Airborne on his shoulder – The Screamin' Eagles, The Widow Makers. They were one of the toughest units the Army had to throw at Charlie. He had obviously seen some action. This was no phony Army drill. The injured dog was also 101st Airborne, which meant he was not only a scout dog, but he was able to jump out of an airplane with a parachute. I had just heard about these new critters that everyone was calling "Super Dogs." This was the first casualty of this new breed. This dog had to be tough to be in the 101st.

"What do we have here?" I yelled over the roar of the blades and engine.

"It's my dog, sir," the young handler replied. "He's hurt pretty bad!" The medevac orderly yelled, "He's lost a lot of blood, captain. We tried to get him to you as soon as we could. Good luck!"

Ding and Dink helped the handler gently lift the large dog from the chopper to the waiting stretcher and move quickly from the helicopter. The Huey made a hasty return to the sky. Helicopter pilots were always in a hurry.

"Be careful with him, guys!" The worried handler repeated, "Be careful!"

Bell and Dow carried the injured dog on the stretcher to the hospital.

"He doesn't look like he's alive," I yelled to the handler above the noise of the Huey.

"He's alive, captain, but he's in bad shape!" the handler said nervously.

From the time Bell and Dow lifted him from the chopper, I didn't see any movement from the limp dog. I could see some kind of crude, dirty bandages covering one of his front legs. The rest of him was shrouded in a green Army blanket. The other thing that was evident from the time the chopper's doors opened was some kind of horrible smell. You got oblivious to a lot of odors in Vietnam, but you never got accustomed to the smell of rotten flesh. We hurried from the chopper pad and down the path to the hospital, through the breezeway, and into the hospital section. J.B. held the door open. Snake and Granny were already inside. We went down the hallway and into the large treatment room.

"Put the stretcher and all on the treatment table, men," I said. "I don't want to move him anymore until I can see what's wrong with him."

I pulled the green blanket down slowly from the dog's head and down the length of his body. He was still breathing. He was a beautiful black and silver color... kind of unusual for a German Shepherd. His left leg was covered top to bottom with layers of gauze and bandage material that were bloodstained and dirty. The stench was even more apparent. J.B. was the first to leave. I think deep down that he was the softest of any of us and couldn't see anything suffer.

"Like, I'm out of here!" he jabbed. "Someone else takes the damn notes. I need my space and some fresh air. This is too heavy for me!" He continued to ramble as he proceeded down the hall and out the door.

"I'll be in the laboratory awaiting instructions, captain, if you need me," followed Snake. "I think my malaria pill is starting to work!"

Porter stood in the doorway, Dink was straight across from me and Ding to one side. The handler stood his distance against the wall.

"What the hell hit 'em?" I asked.

"Some son-of-a-bitch shot him in a hot-damn ambush through his front leg," the nervous handler shouted. "I know he's hurt bad, Doc. I know it!"

It was obvious that a high-velocity weapon had done its job. You could see the leg was dangling from the elbow below the bandages. I'd be lucky to see any leg attached when I removed all the gauze.

"From the smell, it doesn't take a genius to tell that this dog wasn't shot tonight. What was the delay?"

"I know, sir, the handler replied. "He got shot three days ago up in the mountains. The damn monsoons kept the Hueys out and we couldn't get him medevacked till now. We took turns carrying him down the mountain, sharing our food and water. He saved a lot of guys' asses out there. You got to save him, captain. You got to!"

"I'll do what I can." I shrugged my shoulders.

I began peeling the layers of gauze and cotton away from the injured leg. The more I removed, the heavier the stench became. I finally began to remove the last layer of gauze. I carefully began to lift it to reveal the extent of the damage. It stuck to the blood and pus like glue. The leg below the elbow was completely mutilated. A small entrance hole was visible at the point of the elbow no bigger than what a .22 caliber would make, but the high velocity of the M-16 or AK 47 produced an exit hole in the forearm that my two hands couldn't cover. My first thought was that this dog had reached the end of the line.

"Damn, damn, oh shit!" Dinky grunted.

The handler in the back of him looked nervously at the floor shaking his head. When the last gauze wrap was removed, the odor intensified, and Bell left the room. I began to tenderly probe the pus and blood and bone fragments of this huge, gaping wound. Suddenly, without warning, the semi-conscious dog lifted his huge head, growled and snapped, his teeth barely missing my fingers. I reflexively drew back. The handler also jumped up and came over to his friend. He got his first look at the damage.

"Oh God, Paper! They killed you, they killed you! Those rotten bastards killed you!! He screamed as I pulled him into the hallway.

He was practically hysterical. I tried to calm him down. I told him he wasn't helping his dog by losing control. I knew that this kid had already gone through hell. I didn't know what I could say that would calm him down.

"Where you from?" I asked after he calmed down a little.

"Muncie, Indiana, sir," he replied.

"Drop that 'sir' crap stuff. I'm from Hammond," I replied.

"Oh, great, a Region Rat!" He smiled for the first time.

The part of Indiana I was from was called the "Region" and was a collection of cities in Northwest Indiana. There was a fierce rivalry between us and the rest of the state that was mainly rural, especially on the basketball court.

"I went to Purdue," I said almost as an apology.

"That's better, he said. Paper might have a chance."

I shook his hand.

"John Kubisz," I said.

"Tom Hewitt," he replied.

"Now let's see what we can do for your dog," I said. "How about that East Chicago Washington, Kokomo game? The best B-Ball game I ever saw!" I walked back into the treatment room where Dinky was stroking the injured dog's head.

"Kind of a pussy name for a scout dog," Dink said. "Paper."

"And what the hell is Dinky?" Hewitt replied. "The size of your dick?"

"OK men, let's get to work," I said. "This is a mess!"

I started again probing and looking around the wound. Without X-rays, you could see that the radius and ulna were shattered by the bullet. Pieces of bone were everywhere. All the extensor tendons were destroyed (the tendons needed for a dog to place his foot forward). Infection was everywhere. Horrible, green pus oozed from the wound and some bleeding continued. The leg dangled like a limp rag, only attached by a few muscles and tendons.

I looked up at Dinky and shook my head, negatively. Hewitt couldn't see my face blocked my Dow's large frame. He looked over his shoulder at Hewitt, who was starting to feel the total exhaustion of his effort. He was sitting on the floor looking up.

"He's a nice dog," Dinky said, trying to make amends for his name-calling.

"Thanks," Hewitt nodded.

"Take care of Paper for a minute, Dink. I'll be right back. Can I see you in the hallway, Tom?" I asked.

"Tom," I started. "I didn't become a vet to lose patients," I said slowly, watching the agony grow in Tom's eyes. "But, I'm afraid that it's time to say goodbye to Paper."

"No! Doc, NO!! You have to save him!" Hewitt interrupted.

"Even if I could save him, it would mean amputation. I don't think he's going to live much longer. He's almost dead now," I affirmed.

"Please, Doc," Hewitt said quietly, his eyes filling with tears. "Please just try. I don't mind going back to that hell hole, but not without Paper."

I stared back at him, a young man, old before his time, exhausted, trembling. I looked at his best friend on the exam table... more dead than alive. How in the hell could I sentence this dog to death? Whatever it took, I was going to keep this dog alive, despite Army SOP. At least the longer I kept this dog alive, the longer Tom would have to rest, eat and recover to face the inevitable loss of his friend. I continued to stare at Hewitt's face.

"Oh, what the hell. I'll give it a try. They don't call me the miracle worker for nothing," I joked.

That's what Tom needed and wanted to hear. His face came back to life and the color returned to it. I knew I had made the right decision. We went back into the exam room. I told Hewitt to have a seat and I started to get to work.

"Dinky! Get set up for X-rays. Bell! Ding Dong!" I yelled. "Get me a sedative. Snake! Draw some blood for a CBC and a profile and take a culture of this infection," I ordered.

"If you ask me, I should get the post-mortem forms and the specimen jars," Granny replied.

"When I want any lip out of you, Granny, I'll ask for it," I warned. "Someone gets an enema for Granny's mouth," I continued.

"I wish I was in a regular Army unit," Porter replied and walked out mumbling.

I really didn't know even where to begin on Paper. After I gave him a mild sedative, we took radiographs of the radius and ulna. I started a slow debridement... the process of removing dead tissue, bone fragments, dirt, and debris. It was a mess! My old rule of thumb was "when in doubt, cut it out." That meant if you had any doubts about the vitality of tissue, it should be removed. But, in this case, if I started removing everything that looked dead, there wouldn't be anything left to the leg.

Extensor tendons dangled like electrical wires everywhere. Blood vessels and nerves were severed and were scattered like shredded wheat. The rest looked like mush. X-rays revealed the worst fractured foreleg I had ever seen. There was no way to repair this fracture using conventional methods of orthopedics that I learned at Purdue. And then, there was infection everywhere. If I could have seen Paper immediately, at least I could have prevented the infection. No one spoke as I methodically probed, cleaned and cut.

Then, there was still another problem. Not only was this hole the size of two palms, but most of the skin covering this area was also blown away. There would be nothing to sew back together. I knew though, from my experience with Diablo, that wounds will eventually seal off if you could prevent or control infection. A process called granulation.

A lot of the drugs and medications that we used in Vietnam were new and even experimental, like the Keflex we used on Prince. This was the perfect time to try another medication that was just released. This new product contained chloromycetin (a strong antibiotic) and elase (an enzyme that was supposed to eat up dead or necrotic tissue). At the time, I think it cost the Army about $15 a small tube. I dumped about two tubes of this greasy stuff into the crater that was left after my debridement.

Another of my many problems was the fracture and how to immobilize it. I couldn't use a stainless steel pin through the bones which would be the usual technique if this fracture was sterile. I couldn't splint the leg, because these dogs were too powerful to tolerate a splint. The only option open to me was a plaster cast, but how could I put a new one on every day? This infection couldn't be covered for more than a day and Paper couldn't be anesthetized every day to do it. Slowly as I worked, the mechanics of the problem took form.

After applying the CE ointment and lots of gauze pads, I started putting a cast on the leg in a conventional manner. We waited five minutes while the plaster hardened. Then, using a Stryker saw (a saw that has a circular head and vibrates back and forth to cut only hard surfaces like bone and plaster), I cut down one side and then the other, but left the boot part intact around the foot. This provided an envelope type cast that could be removed anytime. I covered it with adhesive tape to hold it in position.

"This dog needs a blood transfusion bad," Snake said, as he entered the room. "His blood count is way down and his white count is over 30,000."

"Bring up Sherman the German, Ding Dong, and tap him for about

500 ml." I ordered Bell.

"Who, or what is a Sherman the German?" Hewitt asked.

"He's the resident flunky who is actually dead. He's worthless but lovable," I replied.

I replaced Paper's lactated ringer's I.V. with Sherman's whole blood and started a slow drip. I was hoping their blood types were compatible because transfusion reactions were common in dogs and there was no way to type them at that time. But everything progressed well and Paper got stronger as Sherman's blood worked its magic.

"He's probably going to walk up to the VC with a limp paw and go 'palsy-walsy'," Ding joked.

"Will he, captain?" Hewitt asked.

"Cut the bull-crap, Ding! Sherman's blood won't have any effect on Paper mentally, but it sure will make him stronger," I said. "I swear, the bullshit around here gets so deep that you need stilts just to get around."

"I'll tell you one thing," Hewitt started. "You're not wimping asses when it comes to blood and gore. Most guys would have heaved their guts out just smelling Paper's leg."

"This? Why this ain't nothin'!" Ding bragged. "We see a lot worse. Tell 'em about the dead guy you saw out at the Air Force Hospital, Doctor J!"

"Don't let Bell bullshit you again, Tom. They don't get any worse than this. I did see one thing worse than this, but it wasn't alive. And since all we to do is watch the blood drip, I'll tell the story one more and final time," I said.

About two weeks before Paper, I had a sentry dog come in that was weak and losing blood internally. We operated on him and removed a large tumor on the spleen that had ruptured. I removed it successfully and had Bell take a section out to the Air Force Hospital's pathologists for a histopath exam to find out what it was and give me some kind of prognosis for the future.

When I didn't hear from them after a few days, I drove out myself. I went into their new pathology building. It looked like something you'd see in downtown Chicago... all new and shiny, but the entire place smelled like a sewer. I kept asking myself, "What the hell is that smell?"

The sergeant at the front desk told me that I could find my report with Dr. Carroll, who was probably in post-mortem down the hall, last door on your left. I proceeded down the hallway and the further I went, the smell intensified. Now, I was never a person who was bothered by odors, but this one left my stomach in a knot and made my nose itch.

I opened the door to what appeared to be a large laboratory… lots of stainless steel tables, microscopes, and test tubes. Three medical type people were standing around a long table that had this large body on it. I thought at first it was some kind of animal, but as I got closer, I could make out fingers and toes. The mystery of the odor's origin was now apparent. I stood there dumbfounded.

"Can I help you, captain?" a voice penetrated my daze.

"Yeah, well, I'm Captain Kubisz from the 764th Med. I sent a sample from a splenic tumor I took off one of our dogs and I was wondering if I could talk to Dr. Carroll," I stammered.

"I'm Dr. Carroll," one of the three announced. "It was an interesting tumor. I'll go and get the report for you. If this bothers you, you can wait up front."

"No, that's OK, I'll wait here," I responded. "I'm used to this kind of stuff."

I really wasn't. This was the sickest mess you can imagine. When Dr. Carroll left the room, I could see the entire post-mortem table. The other two doctors were busily working and taking samples. I was accustomed to the procedure from working on dogs that were KIA (killed in action). A post had to be performed on whatever was left.

"What happened?" I manage to ask.

"This is a flier that got shot down over Da Nang five days ago. They just fished him out of the bay," one nonchalantly said.

The scene before me was grotesque. From his neck to his groin there was nothing left except his back. What was left had swollen from decay and the saltwater. My dad always liked to eat pickled pig's feet when I was a kid, and sometimes I would sample it. But now, all I could think of was how this looked like pickled pig's feet. The buzz of the Stryker saw brought my attention to the one doctor cutting off the cranium to expose the brain. When he had cut completely around the skull, he took a small mallet and tapped the skull until the top came off. The brain, now liquefied from putrefaction, ran down the length of the exam table.

"Make a note… brain, six feet long," he joked.

I couldn't believe it. He actually joked and went about his business as he had probably done a thousand times. I guess if he'd stopped and thought about it, he'd end up in Ward 8.

"What can you tell from a body this decomposed?" I asked.

"We can tell if the explosion occurred inside or outside the plane to rule out sabotage. We can tell who made the weapon that shot him down and we can tell if he had any illegal substance in him," the doctor answered.

"And what do you do with the rest of him when you get done?" I inquired.

"We bag it up and send it home to the next of kin," was the cold answer. "Like what do you think we do with it?"

I couldn't believe it. If this guy was my own brother, I would not be able to recognize him. What a waste of talent, I thought. I didn't have any response to his cold question; I just stood there shaking my head. I could almost feel most of my blood was already out of my face and hands and it wasn't from the air conditioning. Just about then, the door opened and the desk sergeant came in carrying a tray of donuts and sweet rolls.

"Who wants some to go with the coffee I made," he cheerfully asked. At first, I thought he was kidding. By now, I couldn't swallow my own spit. But the other two doctors were unaffected.

"Sure!" said one.

"Great!" said the other, as he shook the remnants of the brain from his slimy gloves and grabbed an empty paper cup. "Put one in here," he ordered.

The sergeant pushed a sweet roll into the cup and the doctor took a bite of it, then a gulp of coffee. That's all it took; my guts were starting to boil and by now, luckily, Dr. Carroll had returned with my report.

"Here's your report, captain. I think you'll find it interesting," Dr. Carroll said, handing me the report.

"Thanks," I said. "Hate to rush, but I have to get back."

I made a quick departure and immediately exited through the rear door. I stood there for a while just breathing the air. I didn't throw up, but I felt like it. Even when I got back to the 764th, everyone thought I looked green and when the story was still fresh, I made everyone else sick.

"Well, that's the story, Hewitt," I completed.

"Makes me hungry just hearing about it, captain," Tom said with a big grin.

By this time, all of us were ready for at least a cup of coffee. We had worked the entire night on Paper and the sun was already rising. Paper's vital signs were stable and he was resting comfortably. We carried him on a stretcher out to the recovery area and placed him across from Sherman. We used a bunch of Army blankets to make a bed. Paper was able to lie on his stomach and was looking around. Everyone stood there looking at him. From the very beginning, every man in the unit felt a closeness to this dog and his handler.

*Paper after his
initial opera-
tion. Hewitt
made sure
Paper was our
first patient of
the day.*

IX.

Hewitt: Thumbs Up – Major: Thumbs Down – Paper: Thumbs Up

"COME ON, TOM, I've got something that will make you sick... Army breakfast!" I laughed. "The Army has the best food in the world until the Army cooks get a hold of it... I wonder what the mystery meat of the week is. Paper will be alright. I'll have Taylor stay with him and if Paper's condition changes, he'll come and get us."

"Sounds good to me, Doc. I don't remember when I ate last," Hewitt admitted. "Even Army food sounds good."

Over breakfast, Hewitt relaxed slightly and told us some of his favorite stories about Paper. There was a time when they were being rocketed outside of Da Nang and he and Paper took cover in the first deep bunker they saw. Then, out of nowhere, some first lieutenant came piling head first into the waiting jaws of Paper. He ran out into the rockets rather than facing Paper. There was another time when his unit captured a VC and began the interrogation. The prisoner kept yelling, *"Khong biet!"* (I don't understand). They brought a growling Paper up to his face and he immediately yelled, "I understand, I understand!" in perfect English.

The stories went on and on. It helped Tom to talk about his only friend in Vietnam, who was now just barely clinging to life. His stories made us all laugh and Tom was the kind of person that we all got along with. But the reality of his poor dog sitting back at the 764th was difficult for me not to think about. Did I make the right decision? Would it have been better if I would have put him to sleep? How would Tom take the news later that Paper was through in the Army?

"How did Paper get shot?" I asked, trying to remove all the doubts in my head.

"We were on patrol and Charlie was everywhere," Tom started. "I told the lieutenant to slow down and give me a chance to work the area with Paper. The jungle was so thick and close that you couldn't see crap. Paper was in front of me only a few feet away, when he went on alert. He alerts like a radar screen… front feet off the ground and he pivots back and forth in the direction of the danger. Some of the guys moved too quickly up the hill and advanced to our right flank, putting us between them and Charlie. When Paper detected the ambush, we were trapped in a cross-fire. It was damn lucky we weren't both killed. Paper might have gotten shot by one of our own men. The whole unit felt bad about Paper….he had saved our asses so many times. Then we couldn't get him out of there because of the damn monsoons and rough terrain. We took turns carrying him down the mountain, sharing what food we had until Paper lost consciousness. He's one hell of a dog!" Hewitt finished.

We were almost in a good mood by the time we returned to the hospital, but the 176th jeep in the drive told me that our old nemesis, Major Kraft, was paying us a visit. Granny had probably blabbed the gory details. He couldn't wait to be the bearer of bad news. Major Kraft stood defiantly in our path. Like some pudgy Napoleonic figure, he stood there with his hands on his hips next to the statue of Snoopy, another cartoon character.

"This Army starts at 0700, gentlemen!" he growled. "Not 0830!"

The men exchanged salutes with him and hurried past to find their own islands of security within the hospital. Bell bravely flipped the major the bird behind his back. If possible, everyone avoided confrontation with the major. I never saluted him when there wasn't any upper brass to impress.

"We've been up half the night with a new arrival, major. A scout dog was shot up in the highlands three days ago. A heck of a nice dog," I said.

"Yeah, sure!" he sarcastically said. "Let's see him. I heard he's mostly dead."

Porter squirmed uneasily behind the major as I gave him a dirty look.

"We're going to have to make this quick, major. As you can see, I've got a sick call and I'm already behind," I said firmly.

The usual collection of sentry dogs and their handlers waited in the breezeway of the hospital after their night patrols. We hurried past them and to the back of the office area where the hospitalized cases were kept. The major stood outside of Paper's run looking at him with a critical eye. Paper lay there looking directly at him and growling. Damn, I thought, this dog is a pretty good judge of character.

"Looks pretty bad to me," the major diagnosed. "What did you find wrong with him?"

I quickly organized my thoughts to minimize the damage. If this clown got one look at the real injuries, we'd have to scrape him off the concrete. I could cover up most of the damage, but I would have to admit at least to the fracture.

"He's taken a bullet to the foreleg and the radius and ulna are broken," I openly admitted.

"Let's see the radiographs," he ordered and started back towards the hospital.

We proceeded through the office area and through the breezeway where the handlers and their dogs were staged. We entered the treatment room, where I had a large X-ray viewer. All the men of the 764th had abandoned us by now, hiding safely in their holes. Hewitt followed nervously behind, probably wondering what kind of a jerk the major was. I retrieved the radiographs wishing I had another set that I could substitute that was less dramatic. Even though the major didn't know shit from Shinola about medicine, he did graduate from some vet school. I casually placed them on the viewer and pointed to the fractures.

"Do you think I'm blind, captain?" he sneered. "That's the worst damn mess I've ever seen! And what the hell is that horrible smell in this dump?"

The major rattled on without waiting for an answer.

"There's not a rat's ass chance in hell that this dog is going to see duty again," he blurted out.

"Put the poor bastard out of its misery and let's get on to something worth saving!"

I could see Hewitt's face turn almost immediately from hope to despair as the major continued to shoot his mouth off.

"I think he's got a chance," I interrupted.

"Don't give me any of your bullshit, captain. I've heard it all before. Again, you are wasting your time and most importantly, the Army's money. If you were under the 176th, I'd order you to dispose of this garbage!" he snapped, then proceeded out of the room in a huff.

Being up all night, a couple of Army pancakes in my stomach, and the look on Hewitt's face, all added up to me blowing a circuit breaker and losing my cool. I caught up the major in the hallway and grabbed him by the shoulder.

"Listen, you arrogant bastard!" I whispered through gritted teeth. "This is my unit and I take my orders from the general in Saigon. In the future, if you have any horseshit comments to make, direct them to the general or blow them out your ass!"

The major was caught completely off-guard and if he wasn't such a little crap, I would have decked him right then. He stared defiantly back at me.

"We'll see, captain!" he smirked. "We'll see who has the last laugh!"

He knew that if I laid a hand on him, my future was over. He turned and proceeded down the hallway briskly and quickly pushed the door open to the breezeway, but maybe just a bit too quickly. A sentry dog and his handler were poised on the other side. As he flung the door open, the dog lunged forward and snapped viciously at the major, damn near nailing him. The major jumped back and placed the door between himself and the sentry dog.

Peeking through the door slit, he bravely yelled, "You'd better learn to control that dog, Mister!"

The cigar chewing handler confidently stood his ground and calmly said, "He doesn't like gooks and he doesn't like brass!"

"And you'd better clean up your act. You're a disgrace!" the major snapped back.

"Right," replied the dirty handler, giving the thumbs up.

"That's 'yes, sir,' private!" the major reminded.

The grubby handler just stood there, staring, his dog growing and moving closer to the major. I think the major realized that most of these guys didn't give a damn about officers and if the handler accidentally dropped his leash, the major's ass was grass! The major inched his way with his back against the wall of the breezeway and around the corner to his jeep. I looked at the dirty handler, gave him the thumbs up and said, smiling, "You're next!"

Hewitt stayed with me through sick call and we compared sentry dogs with scout dogs. He had worked with both but for the last six months, it was only Paper. Practically the only living thing he had been associated with. Hewitt had expanded on Paper's training to include sentry dog techniques. Hewitt was a natural at training animals. There's a certain quality that some people are born with and you can't learn it or train it. Animals know it and respect it. When you combine that certain "it" with the love Hewitt and

Paper had for each other, you have one very special relationship.

"Can that jack-off major make you put Paper away, Doc?" Hewitt asked, as he came back to reality.

"I don't take direct orders from him, but he can make recommendations to my C.O. in Saigon," I said, "Don't worry. If he was a couple ranks higher, he'd be dangerous."

We finished sick call and went out to take another look at Paper. He looked bright and alert when he saw Tom, but was still unable to stand. He made a feeble attempt, but Hewitt quickly told him to take it easy and rest. Tom put a bowl of water in front of him and Paper was able to take a few laps and swallow with some difficulty. Tom kept reassuring Paper that everything would be alright.

"You did a good job, Doc," he said, looking up at me. "When can I feed him?"

"If he's hungry, go ahead and try him on something. The dog food is stored over in that building," I pointed.

"Dog food?" Paper doesn't eat dog food!" Hewitt laughed. "He's used to people food. I got tired of trying to carry enough food on patrol to feed this moose, so he ate whatever I did or whatever we could find in the villages. Sometimes a gook or two!" he laughed again.

"Don't laugh, Doc. Paper's got two kills to his record!" Hewitt confided.

Paper was something extra special. I saw a lot of them come and go, but this dog was different. There was an immediate quality that shone in his eyes, an understanding that is rarely achieved between man and animal. Everyone in the unit could feel it... that certain Karma, like Snake put it. From the first day, we never called him just "Paper." It was always "Paper Dog" or "Mister Paper." There was some kind of human quality that commanded the respect of a first name and a last. But, what did this all mean? Paper's days as a scout dog were over. Maybe his something special made me save him to keep Hewitt from going back to the cesspool of a war he had come from.

"We don't have a lot of gooks around here for Paper to eat and the ones we have are all friendly. I think. Who the hell can tell the difference? But maybe we could round up some bacon and eggs. They throw out more breakfast than they serve. Spare the pancakes. They might kill a normal dog!"

Paper gulped down his breakfast immediately and looked around for more. I told Tom to take it easy since Paper hadn't eaten in a few days, and it was better to feed him every couple hours. Tom sat with Paper all day, talking, napping, and resting with him on the padded concrete run. By that evening, Paper was standing! He could already balance himself on the heavy plaster cast. When I went by the run to check on them, Paper gave a loud bark. Hewitt smiled. Paper wasn't going to die! Hewitt wrapped his arms around Paper and they slept.

The next morning was a bummer for Paper. The sedatives had worn off and the nerve endings in his front leg were again fresh with pain. Tom had to carry him from the run to the treatment room. Paper's face, if a dog had a face, had as much expression in it as any human. One look and you knew the mood he was in… happy, sad, playful, devilish, and in this case, pain. Psychologists have a big word for this phenomenon of giving human qualities to animals. They call it "anthropomorphism." But what the hell do they know, except big words? So-called animal intelligence experts will tell you that dogs are dumb animals. They put a puppy in a cage and raise it in a laboratory and then perform intelligence tests. I'd like to see how intelligent they would be raised in a cage. Anyone that could see Paper for a day could recognize the intelligence of this animal.

Anyhow, Paper was in pain and he looked around at the faces in the exam room as strangers. He gave a low growl that gradually increased in intensity and volume. It was convincing enough to keep everyone at a distance with our hands in our pockets. Hewitt kept hugging Paper and reassuring him that we had saved his life.

"Easy, boy!" Hewitt continued. "Old Doc here is going to remove your cast and check your wound. It's going to hurt some, but he's trying to help you."

"OK Doc. Go ahead," Hewitt urged.

I cautiously approached Paper. This is something I would never attempt with another dog. I have to be crazy, I thought. This dog has two kills to his record and I'll be number three! But Paper laid down and acted like he knew what to expect. As if he was biting a bullet, he let me start removing the adhesive tape from the cast and then the layers of gauze beneath. The wound already looked better. The C-E ointment was doing its job. The culture that we took the day before confirmed that choromycetin was the antibiotic of choice. The dead tissues were being dissolved nicely by the elase. There wasn't any more bleeding and the underlying tissues looked a tad more healthy. But, torn extensor tendons were dangling everywhere. The mere size of the resulting crater was awesome.

"Man, what a hole!" I finally said, breaking the silence.

"How many times have I said that?" Bell quipped.

"How does it look, Doc?" asked Hewitt.

"Taking everything into consideration," I said, "It ain't bad!"

For the next week, Paper had considerable pain, but never let it get him down. Our routine remained the same… Hewitt would carry Paper to the exam room, I'd remove the cast, clean what I could and dump a couple of tubes of C-E ointment in it and recast. Paper continued to get stronger and both Paper and Hewitt gained weight.

About this time, the new port veterinarian arrived to take my old position. His name was Richard "Dusty" Dussel. Within a week, Dusty had already lost his jeep and was pulling his hair out from boredom. And even though he was another Texas Aggie, I invited him to help out around the 764th. I don't know why I got along so well with these Texans; we were always cuttin' each other down. But Dusty should have been a member of the unit because he fit right in. We saw eye to eye on just about everything, especially animal treatment, and surgery. He quickly became familiar with all the cases, including Paper. Both of us knew that Paper required another surgery to remove more damaged tissue and to try to repair some of the extensor tendon damage.

After a week, all of us were almost as close to Paper as Hewitt. We would worry over him like mother hens, but we still had to keep our distance. Paper was kind of reluctant to trust anybody. However, I was able to approach Paper at any time even without Hewitt present. He trusted me and I was getting closer to him. We made the necessary preparations for the coming surgery. This time we had plenty of opportunities to prepare and plan ahead. Dusty escaped the port to assist me. Dink was the second assistant, Bell was on the gas and J.B. provided some Roy Orbison. Paper was sedated and Hewitt carried him into the surgery. Paper was a lot stronger now and we were able to take our time and do a thorough investigation as to the total extent of the damage. Not much could be salvaged from any of the extensor tendons. In fact, several of the opposing flexor tendons had to be repaired.

"How the hell is this dog going to walk without any extensor tendons?" Dusty asked.

"I don't know. Half the things I see around here, I don't believe," I replied. "But look here. The radial nerve is still intact and the main arterial blood supply to the lower leg is good!"

"Shit far!" Dusty said. "How in the cat's hell did this leg get blown apart and the main nerve stay intact?"

We proceeded with the surgery, guided by instinct or some force greater than ourselves. It certainly wasn't by experience. I don't think you could've found anyone with experience in this kind of trauma. Neither of us had any idea on how to close the large opening left from the blast that was devoid of skin. We pulled and stretched what we could from the inelastic surrounding tissues. We were finished in about an hour and I repacked the wound with C-E ointment and replaced the cast. Hewitt carried Paper back to his run and made preparations for another all-night vigil. Dusty and I decided to hit the Officer's Club and tip a few. We sat at the bar discussing Paper and Hewitt.

"What are you going to tell that kid, Hewitt, when he finds out that Paper won't be going back to duty?" asked Dusty.

"I don't know," I replied. "It's going to be harder as time goes by because I've gotten to like them both. They're one hell of a team. But, at least I've taken them out of this war for a while."

"I'm coming out tomorrow morning and see what he looks like," Dusty finished.

The next morning found Paper in exceptionally good shape and spirit. He was not only up, but walking up and down the kennels with Hewitt, barking at the other dogs and at us as we approached.

"Would you look at that!" Dusty exclaimed. "That dog really has some balls!"

"He's one tough S.O.B.!" I agreed.

"You guys gave Paper a new life!" Hewitt happily said.

If it wasn't for the heavy plaster cast, you'd think there was nothing wrong with him. Paper's attitude, according to Hewitt, was like nothing happened. He was bright and alert and kept looking at Hewitt like he was saying, "Let's go! I'm all better!" I warned Tom to take it easy because, despite Paper's willingness to walk and run around, I didn't want him moving too many muscles around that severely fractured leg. We would have enough trouble with the bones mending.

"I'm sorry, Doc. I forgot, "Hewitt apologized. "It's just that he looks so good! We'll listen to your orders from now on. You just do like the Doc says, Paper!" he concluded.

Paper and Tom at Fort Benning, Georgia, for scout dog training together.

Training days. They both look like new puppies, the stress of war still in their future.

X.

Officers Have Privileges

"I AIN'T NEVER SEEN OFFICERS like you two. I was just getting used to Captain K's long hair and tennis shoes and here comes Captain Dusty with longer hair, side-burns, and a shell necklace. Who the hell do you guys know?" asked Hewitt.

"Dusty and I have had it with all this Army bullshit and have officially dropped out!" I said.

"Anybody can be an officer. All you need is uniform. You look like officer material to me, Hewitt."

"Yeah, you could pass for an officer, at least a first lieutenant," repeated Dusty. "That's a good idea. Let's get your ass in an officer's uniform and we can go to the new Army officers' club up on the hill."

"What about me?" asked Bell.

"Me too? asked J.B.

"Ain't nobody goin' to believe you're an officer, J.B. That's pushin' it!" I answered.

We got a couple of sets of fatigues and had one of the mama-sans sew the appropriate patches on for a first lieutenant. Bell and Hewitt stood in front of the mirror admiring themselves like girls going to the prom. Everything was the same on all the uniforms except for the rank patches.

"Lieutenant Bell, I presume," said Hewitt.

"That's First Lieutenant Bell to you, thank you very much!" Bell returned.

"If you ladies are ready, the ball is about to begin!" I proclaimed.

Bell and Hewitt locked arms and skipped out to the jeep. Dusty was called back to the 176th and had to work that night, but he would keep an eye out for the major and colonel and let us know if they were headed our way. Those were the only two that would know Bell and Tom. The new officers' club attracted brass from all over and even visiting dignitaries and civilians. Anyone could look like they belonged.

At first, Ding and Hewitt were a little uptight posing as first lieutenants. They were still under the misconception that officers were special. But after a few beers and looking around at some of the real dip-shits, they relaxed and started enjoying themselves. About eight o'clock, a South Korean band started playing in the main show room. All these groups were about the same, with a couple or three go-go-girls and a singer. They could duplicate the voices and sounds of the popular groups to perfection. And what always amazed me, was most of them couldn't speak a word of English. They did it all by mimicking songs from records they had listened to. What they lacked in talent, they made up in loudness and enthusiasm. Anyway, who was listening; all eyes were glued on the girls. Bell and Hewitt didn't get this kind of entertainment at the E.M. Club!

"Captain Kubisz, telephone call!" came over the P.A. system.

It was Dusty calling to warn me that the major and colonel were on their way. I went back to the table and told Bell and Hewitt that we'd better shake a tail feather ASAP. They both blew kisses to the go-go-girls they had fallen in love with and proceeded through the large, twin doors to the entrance foyer. Bell was on my right side of me and Hewitt on the left. Coming in the opposite direction was a full-bird colonel with starched fatigues and spit shined jungle boots. He was flanked by two other officers. The colonel took one look at us and stopped dead in his tracks.

"Hold it right there, captain!" he yelled.

Oh crap, I thought. The jig is up. Bell and Tom will be arrested for impersonating officers. I'll lose the 764th. Paper is finished without us. We're all screwed.

"Where in the H-E double hockey sticks do you think you're going in them damn dirty tennis shoes?" he asked. "You're a disgrace to the uniform!"

What a relief, I thought! This dude is only worried about my footwear. Another typical jerk-face who thinks he's God's gift to the Army. He's offended by my non-conformance to his aesthetics. Time for my martyr's routine. I reached into my back pocket and handed him my note like some kid giving a note to the teacher from his mommy.

"Well, sir," I started. "It's not my choice. I'm only in tennis shoes because of a war-related injury. I could be stateside, but have elected to finish my work here."

"Yes, sir!" Bell bravely spoke up. "He's practically a fuckin' hero!"

Oh, brother, I thought. Don't get too carried away, Bell. We're not out of trouble, yet. The colonel studied the note forever, folded it and handed it back to me.

"Captain, VC?" he asked.

"Yes, sir!" I replied. "Veterinary Corps, the friendly VC," I said proudly.

"Carry on, captain," he concluded.

"Yes, sir!" I snapped to attention, clicking my tennis shoes together and giving him my best salute.

He started walking away and Bell started in again. "You should have shown him all your medals, captain!"

"I left them all on my other fatigues," I joked.

"You're my hero!" laughed Hewitt.

"Come on, bullshitters, let's get our asses out of here before someone shows up that really knows us!" I urged.

We laughed and joked all the way back to the 764th. We returned late to the compound. Dinky said everything was quiet and he had checked on Paper about a half-hour ago. Hewitt, still joking, walked to the back kennels to give a peek at Paper.

"PAPER!!!" he screamed.

"HELL!" Bell jumped up as we headed out the back door.

"Never mind," Hewitt said, with a sigh of relief. "He was sleeping so soundly, I thought he was dead. He scared the shit out of me, and I scared the crap out of him!"

Hewitt continued hugging and reassuring Paper. This dog would need a lot of TLC before he was able to stay awake for more than a couple of hours. The injury, exhaustion, loss of blood and shock had taken its toll. Even though he looked pretty good, only Dusty and I had the whole picture. I kept cautioning Hewitt and giving him some kind of pessimism just to cool off some of his optimism, and I'm the most optimistic person I know. Tom kept acting like he was back in Indiana and this was nothing more than a pit-stop at the Indianapolis 500. We all stood outside Paper's run and breathed a sigh of relief that nothing else was wrong.

Our anxiety was complicated by another worry. While Holmgren was still the C.O. of the 764th, a mysterious problem developed in the war dogs. For no apparent reason, we would find one with a nose bleed and within a couple of days, he would be dead, despite all efforts to help him. Ray and I could only speculate as to the cause. Maybe some kind of bizarre parasite got up their noses. Maybe it was something in their diets. Or, maybe it was some kind of infection. It seemed to attack our best dogs. A general conference in Saigon concluded that it was a disease, probably carried by ticks. Years later after the war, we would understand it and be able to treat it, but right now, we didn't even have a name for it. We just called it the "Bleeder's Disease."

This disease was the main reason for the military's one-way ticket to Vietnam for these dogs. We had no idea about infecting the population of the dogs in the U.S. It was too deadly to take any chances. We worried about all the dogs, including Paper. The first sign of the disease was a sudden drop in the red blood cell count. All the dogs were tested frequently. My first thought when I heard Hewitt scream was this damn disease had got him.

"It was fun being an officer for a few hours," Hewitt said, getting me out of my deep thoughts.

"Hey, we're not done yet," I said. "I thought we'd all go up to Nha Trang tomorrow. I want to check with some orthopedic specialists about Paper and see if they have any ideas about healing his fracture. Lee has a couple of days off, and Dusty and Suzy want to see Nha Trang anyway."

Dusty and Suzy had become quite an item. When Dusty first arrived in 'Nam, he didn't particularly like the Vietnamese women, until Lee introduced him to this little girl that everyone called "Suzy." Now, he was head over heels in love with her. He found something that was real in these girls that he couldn't find back home. I assured Hewitt that Paper would be alright for the day and we all piled into the three-quarter ton truck and headed for Nha Trang.

Just months before, the 30-mile trip took me over four hours by jeep because the road was so bad. Now, the road was blacktopped most of the way and we made it in about one and a half hours. I usually made the trip once a month to pick up something I needed or get something repaired, like the autoclave (instrument sterilizer). We used it one time to cook a frozen pizza we scrounged from cold storage and it was always getting gunked up. It was also good for baked potatoes.

The first thing that greeted you upon your arrival on the outskirts of Nha Trang was the city dump. Nha Trang was the second largest city in South Vietnam and the city dump spread for miles in every direction right to the edge of town. As far as the eye could see was smoldering rubble with dozens of men, women, and children sifting through the garbage to salvage anything of value or scraps of food. A little community of cardboard boxes served as their homes and they surrounded the dump. Occasionally, when I drove through places like this, I would look over at Lee and she would be crying because these people didn't have it as good as she did. After all, she lived in a permanent shack with a dirt floor.

We drove around the outskirts of the city and went directly to the large hospital and medical supply depot. Everyone waited in the truck while I took Paper's X-rays and went into the orthopedic section of the hospital. I caught all the doctors just finishing their rounds and was able to present Paper's case to them. At first, they shook their heads and shrugged their shoulders. They all had similar cases in people, but present these guys with anything else and they were in another foreign country. Finally, what appeared to be the head honcho spoke up.

"If this were a person, we're looking at a permanent disability. The joint will probably become almost useless. But on the other hand, if this infection isn't under control by now, you might have to cut the whole damn thing off at the elbow," he concluded.

"Great, Doc! I've got some bad news and now I've more bad news. This is a 101st Airborne off-lead scout dog that is worthless unless I can send him back close to 100%," I concluded.

"No way, captain. At best, he's going to have a stiff leg," one spoke up.

I looked around at the others and everyone seemed to be in agreement. I wasn't going to find any miracles here. I thanked them for their time and started back to the truck. I had to regain some composure and put back my face of optimism. At least there wasn't anything that I missed or was doing wrong. I could feel everyone staring at me as I approached the truck.

"Boy! That's a relief," I sighed. "We're doing everything we can and we did everything we should have done!"

"What's Paper's chances? Did they say?" asked Hewitt.

"What the hell do these clowns know about dogs? They can only guess. He'll be alright. Now, let's have some fun!" I finished.

I tried not to get into any lengthy conversation where Tom could pin me down. I'd probably already let some of my confidence slip. I had come to Nha Trang to bolster my own convictions that I had done everything possible for Paper and now it was up to God. Lee and Suzy were anxious to see Nha Trang. Both of them had friends they wanted to visit and Lee wanted to see a movie. The thought of going to see an actual movie, like a real date, was a little different. We drove over to the vet unit area and I borrowed a jeep for the day. Dusty was going to take Bell, Hewitt and Suzy to see the sites.

The only thing that impressed me with Nha Trang, as I drove through the city, was that it was dirtier and smellier than Saigon, if that was possible. One large, continuous slum. Lee directed me through the streets to the main area of downtown. There was one theatre in the large city, and when I saw it, I thought it had been abandoned years ago. All it needed was boards nailed to the outside. People were already lined up for the one daily showing. The price of admission was about 60¢ U.S. – kind of expensive for Vietnam. Kids were half-price, but they had to be able to sit two to a seat. There weren't any popcorn or candy concessions here. You paid the admission and entered directly into the theatre section from the outside. The inside was a lot more frightening than the outside appearance. It wasn't air-conditioned and it reeked with the smell of urine. A couple of ceiling fans slowly moved the hot, humid and smelly air around.

We found our way to somewhere in the middle of the center section. The solid steel, unpadded seat was barely large enough for my American ass, and my knees pushed tightly against the seat in front of me. Within five minutes, I was already uncomfortable. I wanted to take a leak before the movie got started and noticed the Vietnamese word for "Pisser." It was located at the front of the theatre and to the right. Both men and women used the same area. I opened the door and found myself outside in an open urinal. Everybody peed wherever they wanted and there was enough volume to flow back into the building. I finished and found my way back to Lee in a jam-packed theatre.

"This better be a good movie, Lee. This *Dai Uy* has already had it. I'm about to pass out from the stink alone!"

"Be quiet! The movie is starting!" Lee shushed.

So, there I sat watching this movie made in Hong Kong in Chinese with Vietnamese, French and English sub-titles. All Chinese movies are long and sad – and for this American, just about as much fun as pulling teeth. The story, in short, was about a rich Chinese family with two teenage daughters. One was a spoiled brat who made life miserable for her sister, mother and father. Then she finds out that she has cancer and spends what time she has left trying to make up for all her wrong doings. In the end, she's dying – and after two and a half hours of this crap, I'm dying too. Lee and everybody in the whole theatre is crying their eyes out.

I kept thinking... if people in the States could only see this; if these people could only experience a show in the U.S.; if I don't relieve the pain in my knees and ass, I'll be crying with them. I sat there stewing in my sweat and misery. The Chinese broad finally croaks and the agony was over. We filed out of the theatre, Lee drying her eyes and telling me what a great movie it was. I kept shaking my head and rubbing my knees and ass. Lee couldn't believe that I didn't like the movie. I assured her that it was my first and last movie in Vietnam.

"Will you take me to see one of my old friends who lives not far from Nha Trang?" Lee asked coyly.

It's funny how we sometimes put our foot in our mouth. Lee started directing me through the streets of Nha Trang and before I knew it, we were in the country and a good distance from town. She'd tell me to turn here, then turn there, and it wasn't long before I was on some God-forsaken dirt road, in the middle of nowhere, with the jungle close to each side of the jeep. Suddenly, a group of armed men appeared in front of us.

"Shit, Lee! Those are VC and we are in some heavy trouble!" I warned.

I thought of my .45 that I had at my side. It was a pea-shooter compared to an AK-47. They looked almost as surprised as we did. What the hell was this American captain doing out here? Lee kicked into high gear and started rattling off her Vietnamese in some kind of frantic mood. I knew enough Vietnamese to make out what she was telling these guys, who now had their weapons pointed right at me.

Lee told them that I was the number one doctor who helped the Vietnamese on his own, even the VC and that there was a mother having a baby and I was her only hope. It looked like they were buying it and I started turning the jeep around. One of the men told the others that he had heard of me. The others studied the insignia on my lapel. They were the same as a medical doctor's, except for the "V" printed over the caduceus. Lee kept talking and thanking them while I kept edging the jeep out of there. Within a short distance, they disappeared into the jungle behind me. The gravity of the possibilities raced through my head. We were damn lucky.

"Damn it, Lee! Don't ever pull this crap again. You could have gotten both of us killed!" I ranted.

"I'm sorry, honey," Lee said quietly.

"First you torture me in some hell hole called a movie! Then, you drag me all over creation and we meet your local order of VC who just happens to be friendly. I have to be nuts to have a girl give me directions. Never again!!" I raved.

"I'm sorry!" Lee repeated.

Lee had a way of arguing. Hell, it was more my fault than hers. There was a war going on and sometimes you needed a reminder. Another example of being in the wrong place at the wrong time. Vietnam only reinforced my opinion that when you're called by the man upstairs, it doesn't matter where you are or what you are doing, it's all over. I believe that all of us have a mission and everything we do has a purpose. We headed back to Nha Trang and our rendezvous with the others. Hewitt and Bell were bursting with excitement over their afternoon with Dusty and Suzy. They had gone to some Vietnamese club that Suzy knew and saw a show that featured a five-piece band and eight strippers.

"Man, I wish the guys back at Cam Ranh could see this show!" Bell commented.

"I could arrange that. You pay the price and they will come," Suzy said.

Dusty and I looked at each other. By now, our diabolical minds were working as one. We met with the group's manager and found out that we could have them for one performance for $300. We figured at $10 a head, we wouldn't have any trouble finding thirty guys at Cam Ranh to chip in. The only drawback was we had to provide transportation and get the necessary permits to the peninsula. Dusty could borrow one of the 176th's three-quarter ton trucks and the 764th had the other. Screw the necessary permits. I knew most of the M.P.s and I'd arrange to have Captain Loganberry meet them at the check-point and OK their admission. To cover our asses, we would invite all the C.O.s from the base, including the Base Commander himself. We'd tell them it was just another USO show. We returned to Cam Ranh and made the necessary preparations.

XI.

King MOOO and The Strip Show

I'm sure Bell and Hewitt enjoyed being officers for a couple of days. Hewitt fit right in to this group of anti-Army rebels. All of us were single, with no real attachments back home and all our futures were in question. As I drove back from Nha Trang, I kept thinking about the grave prognosis all the doctors had given Paper. How could Hewitt exist without Paper or Paper without Tom? How could Hewitt leave Vietnam without his best friend? The Bleeder Disease stopped any dog from returning, even if he was crippled.

The next day was blood testing day and everyone was busy making preparations to test all the dogs, including Paper. After the first two weeks, Paper had accepted everyone at the 764th including Granny but still looked to Hewitt for assurance and trust. A simple blood test was nothing for Paper; you didn't even have to hold him steady. However, for the other 120 dogs at Cam Ranh, it was an endurance marathon that lasted most of the day.

Each dog was muzzled and held on a table outside in the back of the hospital runs. It would take about five men to hold one down. I would brace myself, insert the needle in a customary manner and the dog would buck and fight until the needle was out of the vein. Sweat would roll off our faces and patience would wear thin.

"You know, Captain K," the colonel belched. "I've always had an idea about taking these blood samples."

While we were engrossed with our blood-letting torture, the colonel had managed to penetrate our perimeter defenses and was now standing behind us giving his cool critique of what we were doing wrong. I doubt if he had ever taken a blood sample since vet school.

"I can hardly wait to hear this shit!" I muttered to one of the M.P.s, my back to the colonel.

"What's that?" the colonel asked. "I couldn't hear you over these growling dogs."

"I said I'd appreciate any suggestions," I smirked.

"Well," he pondered," the blood is actually running in the veins back to the heart; and we are putting the needles in the opposite direction to the blood flow. If we would turn them around and insert them towards the paws, the blood would be flowing directly into the syringe."

I stood there starring at him, mouth opened, sweat running down like a shower. I couldn't believe he was serious. I looked for some glint in his eye, some subtle smile, but nothing. This jerk wasn't kidding. I finally got my voice back and stepped away from the table.

"You want to show me how in the hell that could be done on this animal, sir?" I asked sarcastically.

"That's your job, captain," he smiled. "I'm just here to make suggestions. I came out here looking for Captain Dussel. He's spending too much time away from the port. And what's this request for one of our three-quarter ton trucks?"

"Captain K needs a ton of supplies from Nha Trang and I thought we could help him," Dusty spoke up.

"Just this one time. I'm going to Hong Kong on R&R tomorrow and I'll be gone for a week. The major is in charge until I get back. I don't want to hear any crap from him when I get back. Carry on," he finished and departed.

"If he only knew the truth!" I said. "Bring me the last dog. Tom, take Paper over to the treatment room so I can work on him when I get done."

Paper was the ideal patient. In orthopedics, I always said half depends on the vet and the other half depends on what the dog will let you do. Paper and most other dogs can easily chew their stitches out, or even chew through a plaster cast. I witnessed dogs chewing open abdominal incisions and eating their own guts. But with Paper, Hewitt could tell him something and Paper would obey. Paper never even tried to lick his cast. We could all talk to him as if he understood every word we said.

The improvement in Paper's leg was truly unbelievable. The bones were mending nicely with a strong callus developing. There was no sign of infection. The hole was still very large, but a good granulation bed had developed at the bottom of it. Reflexes in the paw were excellent, but muscle control was difficult to evaluate because Paper remained in the cast at all times and most of the muscles were in some state of atrophy (the shrinking of a muscle due to not being used). We were putting the last strip of tape on the cast when Taylor came bursting through the door in his usual manner.

"Captain, come quick!" King MOOO has got another handler!" he yelled.

Just the very sound of his name would make anyone's blood run cold that knew him – "King MOOO"! This was the "Vietnam Wacko" of the sentry dog world. His given name was "King" and the tattoo in his ear was M-OOO, hence King MOOO (like a cow). He was the biggest of all the dogs I saw in 'Nam, weighing in at 135 pounds and we're not talking couch potatoes! Somewhere down the line, his circuits had become crossed and he wasn't out to make friends and influence people. He was prone to uncontrollable fits of rage for no apparent reason. This dog was always in some stage of meanness. His first handler had been killed in action working with King and from that time on King progressively got worse. Despite the obvious danger, a lot of handlers wanted a crack at him. King MOOO became a status symbol – the biggest, meanest sentry dog in the whole Army. Most handlers didn't get past the first day's training without King MOOO nailing them. Most were too afraid to continue after a few days. But then, it looked like King had met his match. A new batch of handlers had arrived and a few drew straws for King. The winner was an excellent dog handler and I thought he might have a chance. The sergeant gave him strict instructions about King and how dangerous and unpredictable he could be.

"Watch your ass and don't take any chances with this bastard!" the sergeant repeatedly warned.

Daily, the new handler would approach King MOOO with food and water. And daily, King would savagely throw his 135 pounds against the door of his kennel. The handler patiently – and in complete control – began to gradually wear King down to where he could be approached. This procedure was similar to other sentry dogs, but this handler achieved apparent success faster than I had seen before. The handler was finally able to bravely open the run and make contact. He could apply the bite-proof muzzle and take it off again. Each step progressed methodically and with caution. After about a week, the handler was able to work King with the bite-proof muzzle in place. The first week's training was uneventful while the muzzle was in place.

There was nothing wrong with King's intelligence but something upstairs was burned out.

Then the crucial second week of training without the muzzle began. The first two days were like watching a different dog. King performed better than any dog at the 981st. The handler was firm, but King was compatible. And now on the third day, Taylor was telling me that the old King MOOO had returned. We dropped everything we were doing. Hewitt yelled to Paper to stay and we all ran out of the hospital. King was on top of his handler, viciously attacking him. The handler lay motionless, not making a sound. The sergeant had already grabbed the leash as I approached and yelled.

"KING!! OUT!! NO!!! I screamed.

My immediate thought was – who's next? This dog could have easily turned on the sergeant, then me. There would be no way to stop him without a bullet. But as suddenly as he attacked, he stopped. I told the sergeant to put him in the first open run that he could find and do it as quickly as possible. My eyes followed him until King was in a cage. As soon as the door was shut and locked, King turned and attacked the door. My next concern was for the handler, still not moving or making a sound.

I ripped open his fatigues and could see large, gaping holes across his abdomen and chest. None of them were bleeding but the handler was now gasping and turning blue. He was in profound shock, and if we didn't act quickly, he'd be dead. The Air Force Hospital was seven miles away over bad roads and we might not have enough time. What would I do if this were a dog? I ran back to the hospital, grabbed a syringe and put a cc of epinephrine in it. I ran back and quickly stuck it in the handler's arm. We loaded him into the jeep and headed across the dunes to the hospital. By the time we arrived, the shock was subsiding and the handler was again coherent. He would recover from his wounds physically, but he would never be able to work with the dogs again. He put in for a transfer to a different unit.

An incident like King's attack would put everybody on edge, including the other dogs. Knowing what these animals could really do if given any chance was just a little bit unsettling. The other dogs would always be uptight any time one of them went on a full-blown attack.

Preparing for the upcoming strip show was the best thing to get everybody back to normal. This project would take some luck and a lot of planning. I was in charge of the operation once they got to Cam Ranh, and

Dusty would handle it from Nha Trang to Cam Ranh. Selling the tickets to the first 30 guys was the least of our problems. I had J.B. type up some invitations to the head cock-knockers at the base using Transcommand stationary so it couldn't be traced. I made arrangements with my friends at the motor pool to set up a stage in the back of their large garage to block it from passing view.

Captain Loganberry would be at the check-point all day and wait for Dusty to return with the girls. Dusty's part of the trip had the most risk. If he were stopped along the way, he didn't have authorization for the Vietnamese nationals that he was escorting. Everything was in place and the big day had arrived. Dusty headed for Nha Trang early in the morning, driving one three-quarter ton truck while Bell and Hewitt drove the other. I paced all day long worrying about them getting stopped. If everything went according to plan, they would arrive at the check-point at about 4PM.

That time came and went. By now, it was 5PM. I kept calling the check-point and my worries were joined with the worries of Captain Loganberry. Everything was in place for the show. The troops were already in position for the best seats. We reserved the front row for the VIPs. The beer and liquor were flowing freely. The show was slated to start at 7PM. and it was already close to that. Finally, the silence was pierced by the phone ringing.

"They're on their way!" Loganberry announced. But I don't know how Dusty is driving. He's barely able to walk, he's so drunk. Bell and Hewitt aren't much better. I'm going with them to the motor pool."

I hopped into my jeep and flew to the motor pool. I knew that the troops would be ready to tear the place down by now. I had already sent Dow ahead to tell them that there would be a delay, but I knew he had run out of excuses by now. The place was jumpin' when I arrived. All the seats were filled. Everybody was chanting.

"Bring out the girls… Bring out the GIRLS!!"

"We want to see some skin!"

The VIP row remained empty and I could see the top brass standing in the back, afraid to mix with the 30 E.M.s that bought tickets. One of them was talking to Major Kraft and pointed to me when they saw me arrive. The secret was out and everyone knew that it was Dusty and me who arranged this whole thing.

"How's it goin', major?" I bravely said as I approached him.

"Cut the crap, captain! You know how's it goin'. Where the hell is Captain Dussel? His ass is going to pay for this!" the major steamed.

The major didn't have long to wait for his answer. The three-quarter ton trucks were pulling up to the back of the motor pool and Dusty, Bell and Hewitt were stumbling towards me. The girls and the band headed for the dressing room we had set up. Dusty was only dressed in his fatigue pants and had a pair of rubber shower thongs on his feet.

"What the hell happened to you guys?" I asked a blurry-eyed Dusty.

"You don't even want to know! We worried about getting stopped by the M.P.s in the Nha Trang area and the fuckin' South Vietnamese militia stopped our gonads. We had to go to their headquarters and put a show on for them before they let us go. We're lucky to get here!" The words slurred from Dusty's mouth.

Dusty was totally oblivious to the major who stood there taking in every word. The major, by now, was glaring at him. I motioned to Dusty that the major was standing right next to him.

"How's it goin', major. Glad you could make the show," Dusty said, giving the major a sloppy salute.

I quickly went up to the stage and grabbed the microphone.

"May I have your attention, please? Sorry for the delay, but the show will get started in a minute. I'd like to ask the guests of honor to be seated in the front row. The show will be worth the wait," I assured them.

The band was already set up and started playing some rock and roll. Everybody jockeyed for position to get the best view of the stage and just about everybody had a camera or movie camera. Then, after the first couple of songs had begun to settle the troops, the first girl paraded out to the shouts and cheers of the crowd. She performed a modest strip tease and the brass in the front row seemed to be enjoying themselves along with everyone else. I stood alongside the stage with Dusty, while Major Kraft stood way in the back of everyone.

As each girl took her turn, their performances got more and more outrageous than the one before. Then it was two at the same time, then three. While the girls were performing, I went into the dressing room and told the manager to make sure that the VIPs in the front row got the royal treatment. By the third or fourth act, each VIP got more than they bargained for. One of the girls took a pair of glasses from one colonel and stuck them in her G-string, refusing to give them back unless he removed them with his teeth. Another had his face smothered between a large set of boobs. By now, several VIPs had gotten so embarrassed they had gotten up and retreated to the rear and were talking to Major Kraft who glared in my direction.

Dusty was practically in a state of coma, standing there numb, a half bottle of scotch at his side. By the time the grand finale started, all the troops were whipped to a frenzy. All eight girls appeared on stage at the same time and started dragging some of the guys on stage. One grabbed Dusty, pulled him by his pants and then proceeded to remove them. Like a lot of other guys, he didn't wear anything under them and when they dropped, the glare of flashbulbs was blinding. She proceeded to get on top of him, but he was too blown away to do anything except watch. The noise was deafening! I knew all the effort was worth this result. Most of these guys, especially Hewitt, had very little chance to see girls or even relax and just let go.

I know everybody certainly got their money's worth. The front row, however, was totally wasted on the highbrow brass. I don't think these guys could relax if you gave them a sedative. In fact, a couple of them looked downright mad. The final G-string was removed and the show was over. Everyone left in an orderly manner, but I could see Major Kraft waiting and sneering as I tried to get Dusty and the girls hustled out of the area. The major pushed his chubby body through the men trying to leave and cornered us by the dressing room. Dusty stood waving in the breeze.

"Not so fast, captains!" he shouted. "Your asses are finally in some trouble you can't get out of. I've got you on enough charges to send you up the river for a few years: unauthorized use of Army vehicles, unauthorized transport of Vietnamese Nationals, pornography, etcetera, etcetera, etcetera. Now, I want you to report to my office in the morning and you, Captain Dussel, report immediately to my office!"

While the major was ranting, Dusty stood there swaying to and fro. I doubt if he heard a word. But when the major ordered him to report to his office, Dusty came to life. He pushed his pie-eyed face up to the major's.

"Fuck you, major!" he proclaimed. "I'm going home with one of these fine girls!"

I looked back at the major. He looked like a thermometer ready to explode. I knew Dusty was totally out of his gourd by now.

"It's OK, major," I interrupted. "He's slightly under the influence.

I'll make sure he's in your office first thing in the morning."

The major stood staring at Dusty, then turned to me.

"You make sure you're both at my office at 0900. You may not be in my unit, but by the time I'm finished with you, you might be!" the major quipped.

"Yes, sir! We'll be there!" I snapped. "You can count on it!"

I probably was lucky not to have been drinking with Dusty. I would have been in the same situation. At least, one of us was in control to take care of the other and to make sure the girls got back to Nha Trang in the morning. As I expected, the next morning found Dusty totally unaware of most of the previous day's happenings. After I filled in the blanks for him, he was sure we were both headed for Leavenworth. He reported as ordered to the major's office while I paid a visit to a friend at the AG (Adjutant General) office – the legal eagle. I filled him in on all the details. He was already aware of the show the night before. The word had spread quickly and he was disappointed that he hadn't been there. We had a nice long conversation that was very illuminating and gave me all the ammunition I needed to face the major. By the time I entered his office, my confidence had been completely restored.

"Captain Kubisz reporting as ordered, sir!" I came to attention; he thought he had me over a barrel.

"Captain Kubisz," he slowly started. "You and Captain Dussel, who just left here, are confined to quarters until I can figure out what appropriate punishment will be administered. And I want —"

"Excuse me, sir," I interrupted. "I don't think so. I made a stop at the AG's office before I got here and I learned some very interesting things.

"First of all, you can't take any disciplinary actions against an officer without a court martial. Secondly, acting as C.O. of the 176th, this would be one hell of a black mark on your record. Thirdly, if anybody has any punishment, there are a dozen guys who are going to be very upset. So upset, they might want to send some pictures or movies back home to the wives of those VIPs that sat in the front row. Now, I think it's time for bygones to be bygones. After all, boys will be boys!"

The major sat there dumb founded. What could he say? I took him completely off guard. He almost had to come out and admit he didn't have a leg to stand on.

"You're a bit too cocky for your own good, captain. But I've already been contacted by the Base Commander, who expressed some of the fears you just mentioned. He doesn't want any charges placed and would like the whole matter to be dropped. A new C.O. will be here shortly and I don't want any trouble either. So, if I have your assurance that this will not happen in the future, the subject is closed," he requested, trying to regain some sense of decorum.

"Yes, sir!" I said. "Never again!"

I left the office trying to hide a smile and trying not to literally yell out loud. I went by the BOQ, where Dusty was sent to serve his confinement.

I walked in like a whipped puppy and stared at Dusty, who looked like the night after.

"We're in deep shit, right?" he asked.

"That's right, Dusty," I mournfully relented. "They're going to send us to… to…"

"To where — To WHERE?" he raged.

"To Vietnam, Texas Aggie!" Then I started breaking up.

We had successfully pulled off this potential fiasco and again had beaten the brass at their own game.

XII.

A Montage of the 764th

BY NOW, THE 764TH had coalesced into an exclusive, private club. Everyone else was an outsider and we liked it that way. The final membership of this fraternity included the men of the 764th (Dinky, Ding Dong, Snake, J.B. and Granny) with additional privileges extended to Hewitt, Dusty and Taylor. They were the best in the United States and I was proud to be in their numbers.

The 764th became home and our private club house. In the evenings, we sat around drinking beer and playing cards. Snake remained a loner and many times would be off in the hillsides doing his own thing, smoking grass or looking for some weird critters to add to his bizarre collections.

Among the dozens of oddities that Snake had collected were some that were poisonous. He kept a cobra in one of our bunkers and a bamboo viper in a box on a filing cabinet in the office. On one of the major's routine visits, he noticed the sign on the small wooden box: "DANGER! DO NOT TOUCH! POISONOUS SNAKE INSIDE!!" The major stood in front, reading the sign.

"What are you guys hiding in here... some illegal dru —."

Before he finished his sentence, he began to open the top despite rapid and repeated warnings from everyone in the office. As he quickly opened the top, a small green snake coiled back, poised to strike. He quickly slammed it shut. I yelled for Snake and the major tried to pull himself together.

"That's a bamboo viper, that is," the major stammered.

"Very good, major, that is a bamboo viper," Snake announced as he entered the office.

The major regained some of his composure.

"That's what they call a damn 'two-stepper'... the first step, it bites you; the second step, you're dead!" the major muttered. "You're going to kill someone around here with this crap!"

"They're not all that dangerous, major," Snake reassured him, "Unless you are a very sensitive person to their venom."

Snake then opened the box and with his bare hands, lifted the small snake and held it up for examination. It almost didn't look real; it's wire-like body flexing; it's red eyes like glass.

"Put that damn thing back in that box right now, Mister," the major warned. "This is an Army unit, or at least it's supposed to be – not some damn zoo!"

The major had lost whatever cool he thought he had and made a rapid exit. He would never again be curious about what was in our boxes or cabinets. In fact, his snooping any drawer, chest, refrigerator or desk was history.

Snake Terwillerger had his own private world within the world of the 764th. It included his grass and critters and excluded the rest of us from either. He walked that thin line between reality and the *Twilight Zone* – between a genius and a space cadet. His friends included a nine-foot reticulated python, a seven foot Asian rat snake and an assortment of three to five inch centipedes, spiders of all creation and many unnamed, unclassified things that were straight out of a science fiction book!

I saw Snake injured only twice by his friends. Once he captured a huge centipede as it crossed in front of us while we were by the dog runs.

Snake grabbed it and it bit his hand. He dropped it and the centipede ran inside his pants leg and up his leg. Snake stopped its progress at the knee and it bit him again. The centipede then ran back down, where Snake captured it and rushed it off to his laboratory. Almost immediately, his leg was numb up to his groin and his arm to his shoulder. He refused treatment and said the condition was only temporary.

Another time, his Asian rat snake escaped in the laboratory. This is a non-venomous snake, but what it lacks in poison, it makes up in aggression. The seven foot snake shot up one side of the lab and bit Terwilliger again and again. You never heard so much commotion from Snake's normally quiet lab. Cut and bleeding everywhere, he eventually caught the reptile and returned it to its cage.

Once Taylor came into my office and asked if Terwilliger had any pets on growth hormone. There was a snake in the concertina wire tool that looked about 20 feet long.

"You want to see it?" Taylor asked.

"No!" I said sarcastically, "and I'll bet you've been sampling some of Snake's secret stash!"

"Honest, captain. If you don't believe me, I'll show you." Taylor urged.

Taylor led me and a few others outside to the back of the 981st M.P. where the sand met the tall grass. As luck would have it, Snake was on R&R and wasn't available. As we approached the concertina wire, the outline of a pipe-like silhouette appeared. As we got closer, you could see that it was a snake. The concertina wire was six feet high and this snake's head was above it. The rest stretched out along the ground...about eighteen feet in all!

"What the hell kind of snake is it?" I asked.

"That's the biggest mother I've ever seen!" said Bell.

Someone picked up a rock and threw it at the poised snake. The snake immediately came to life and arched backwards, flaring the skin below its head... the unmistakable hood of the great king cobra. I had learned from Terwilliger that this was the most deadly of all the land snakes in the world. One bite could easily kill an elephant. The snake reeled and disappeared in the tall grass, scattering us in all directions. We had never given much thought about running around the compound at night. We always felt pretty secure with all the dogs around, but from that day on, we were all afraid to walk around the compound at night. Every time someone had to take a piss, they carried a flashlight.

About the funniest story involving snakes occurred one day when a lieutenant colonel arrived at our compound unannounced. Hanging from his hand was a four foot, black, yellow and green snake that was already dead.

"I understand you have some sort of a snake specialist out here," he inquired.

"Yes sir," I replied, Spec. IV Terwilliger. He's the best. I'll get him for you."

"All I want to know is if this thing is poisonous," he said, holding the snake up to view. " I was going to take a crap and the damn thing bit me on the ass!"

I don't know how any of us kept from crackin' up right then, but this guy was so serious. Snake identified it as a non-venomous species and the colonel, now relieved, departed still carrying the snake. I often wondered if he ever got his job done or if a snake biting you in the ass stops all bodily functions. Or, is the process speeded up? I'll bet one thing – he will always look before ever sitting down again. I know I did!

It was the fourth week of Paper's hospitalization. His progress was phenomenal, for lack of a better word. One morning during a sick call, I could no longer quell my curiosity. I examined Paper's leg, its deep hole still in the progress of granulation, but the shattered radius and ulna were almost completely healed. The make-shift cast worked like a charm, mainly due to Paper's tolerance. The beautiful callus was holding the bones together, although it was still slightly soft. Everyone was standing around as usual to get my prognosis of the day. I made my big announcement.

"I want to see what Paper does without the cast. Hewitt, gently and softly, put him on the floor," I ordered.

Hewitt, wide-eyed, stared at me almost in disbelief. No one said a word. You could hear the proverbial pin drop. Paper faced his first big step since the operation. Was the leg functional at all? Could he even put any weight on it? Tom slowly lifted Paper off the exam table and gently placed him on the floor. The atrophied and battered leg just hung there like a piece of dead meat. My heart fell from my throat to the floor with Paper. I could feel my emotions shrink within me. The leg was damaged too severely to recover… too many nerves and tendons were destroyed. Paper looked at Hewitt. Hewitt looked at me. He must have seen that I could no longer hide my feelings. I think I must have had the same look and feel when I witnessed the dead guy at the Air Force Hospital. I stared back at Tom, my eyes telling the whole story.

"What do you want him to do, Doctor J?" Hewitt broke the silence that filled the room like a morgue.

I couldn't answer. I just looked back at Hewitt.

"Come on, Paper! Walk to Captain K!" Hewitt urged.

Paper took a step. The leg was lifeless. He took another. It looked like it moved slightly. Then he took another and another. By the fourth step, Paper brought the leg forward and some invisible force actually moved the paw and placed it weakly on the floor! The emotions began to grow like some kind of slow explosion that you could feel building in intensity until it couldn't be contained in silence any longer. I knew that everyone was in tune to what I was feeling. It started as a slow roar and grew until we were all yelling, screaming, dancing and jumping. Paper started barking. The noise was loud enough to carry through the hospital and across the breezeway to the office area, jarring Granny from his desk.

"What's going on?" he meekly peeked into the exam room.

Dinky grabbed him and started dancing in the hallway with him.

"It's Paper, you old fart-ass. He can walk!" yelled Bell.

Dusty looked at me. Perhaps only he understood from a medical point of view, what we were watching. The other guys worried and wondered, but Dusty's education entitled him to the knowledge that this was more than a dog just walking. We were being witnesses to a miracle. Paper defied all explanation from a mere medical aspect. We might have saved Paper's life – and maybe we saved what was left of his leg. But, that he could use the leg, extend it forward and then walk on it, was not possible. Both of us stood in silence shaking our heads and smiling.

"How in a cat's ass can this dog extend that poor leg?" Dusty commented. "What the hell is left?"

"I learned a long time ago, Dusty, that they can't teach it all in vet school," I said. "Sometimes the man upstairs has His own ideas!"

Praying was something I don't think we ever discussed in the Army, but I'm sure most of us did it. And if you didn't know the "Man Upstairs," then you got a quick introduction to Him in 'Nam. Basic training should have included prayer instruction. I know I prayed and I'll bet Hewitt prayed too, because something had happened beyond the wonderful world of medicine.

It took the rest of the morning just to come down from the high we were on.

I gave Hewitt instructions to increase Paper's exercise as much as possible. Even though the cast had to remain on the leg for at least another week, I wanted Paper to exercise the muscles and tendons in that leg to prevent adhesions of these structures while the calcification of the bones was taking place. Paper could have free run of the entire 764th compound if he wanted. It was time for Paper to play, and play he did!

Paper's newfound freedom brought all of us even closer to him. He recognized each of us as his friend and would run from one to the next. Even Sherman the German got into the act. They seemed to have their own sense of communication. Maybe it was the fact that they spent four weeks in opposing kennels and got used to seeing each other. Or maybe there was a bit of truth in what Dinky joked would happen if we gave Sherman's blood to Paper. For whatever reason, they were friends taking turns chasing each other around the compound. The Rambo of German Shepherds and the Pee Wee Herman of German Shepherds, playing in Pee Wee's Playhouse.

Sometimes at night when no one was around, I would sit with Paper in my office, talking with him. It's funny how we can sit and talk with a dog, but sometimes that's easier than talking to a person. I think dogs are the best four-legged psychologists in the world. They certainly are the best listeners. I could entrust my most personal secrets with Paper, assured that he would faithfully keep them.

There were many things that I still couldn't tell Hewitt. The best I could hope for was to send Paper back to Okinawa to be used to train new dogs, as we had done before with other dogs. Maybe I could even get Hewitt transferred with him. But no matter what, Paper was through as a war dog. The hole in his leg would take months to heal and would be prone to injury again if there was a large scar on it. Scar tissue becomes very easily damaged by anything, even blades of grass. I shared Paper's destiny only with him.

"Don't be too jealous, Paper, but I'm going to have Tom work with another scout dog tomorrow," I told Paper one evening.

A few days before, I had a scout dog named Gunga come in after his handler was killed in action. I thought, foolishly, that maybe I could get Hewitt interested in another dog. Gunga was an exceptional, well-trained dog and maybe Hewitt would develop some attachments to him. The next morning after sick call, I told Hewitt to come out to the kennels.

"I'd like you to put this dog, Gunga, through his paces, Tom," I said," just so he doesn't get too rusty."

They worked beautifully together out of sight of Paper. Hewitt could make any animal perform to the best of their abilities. He could look deep into their hearts and pull out that extra something that no one else in the world could do. Only animals could recognize this kind of person and respond accordingly.

"He's a good dog, Doctor J," remarked Hewitt, "but he's a long way from being Paper."

"Maybe it will just take some time," I retorted.

"No, he's OK, but he'll never be a Paper Dog," Tom assured me.

Well, I thought, that idea went down the toilet. There was no way I could find any dog to come close to Paper. By now I had seen hundreds of dogs in Vietnam and a lot of them very good and a few exceptional ones. But Mister Paper was a notch above any of them. I would have to count on something else to make Tom realize that Paper couldn't return to active duty with him.

The next morning, Dinky, Bell, J.B., Hewitt and I were standing in the breezeway between the hospital and the office area. Bell was rough-housing with Paper... putting him in a bear hug from side to side.

"You're not so tough, Paper Dog," Bell taunted. "You're just a big pussy cat!"

"He's right, Tom," I said, seeing my chance to show Tom that Paper wasn't going back to duty.

"Paper looks more like a house pet than a fierce war dog."

"You think so, Captain K?" Hewitt said. "Watch this."

Hewitt grabbed Paper's collar and held him tightly. He then pointed at Bell.

"Get ready to run for your life, Bell," Tom announced. "Gook! Paper, GOOK!" Hewitt yelled, pointing to Bell and then releasing Paper.

Paper sprung forward growling and barking at Bell. Bell took off running as fast as he could with Paper hot on his heels, slowed only by his heavy cast. The frantic expression on Bell's face as he tripped and jumped around the compound left us all laughing to the point of tears. If Bell wasn't a good runner, Paper would have caught him even with his heavy cast.

Around and around Bell ran, screaming for his life like in some comic movie. I finally regained some composure and told Hewitt to call Paper back before Bell tripped or something and Paper ate him.

"Paper, STOP! Friend!" yelled Hewitt, still laughing.

It was over as quickly as it started. Bell gave Paper a hug and all was forgiven. I had lost another chance to tell Hewitt the news I kept inside. Everybody's spirits were too high for me to put a damper on them. That evening, Dusty wanted me to meet him at the officers' club and the men wanted to get a case of beer and party at the 764th. I told them it was alright with me if they partied, but to keep an eye out for the major because I hadn't seen him for a couple of days.

Dusty and I usually sat at the club until it closed and Lee and Suzy got off work. But that night, Lee went home early because her baby was sick and I couldn't see just sitting around with Dussel. I decided to drive back to the 764th and get into a poker game, at least. It was about 10PM.

I had rarely ever seen another vehicle on my five mile drive back to the hospital, but in front of me, I could see the lights of a jeep headed for the 764th. I sped up to just in back of it.

My suspicions were correct and I could make out the insignias of the 176th Vet. It was Major Kraft. There was no way to warn the troops that trouble was on the way. The road split the 764th from the POL tanks and as I looked over to the hospital compound, I couldn't see a single light. Either there was a power outage, or someone had already tipped them off as to the major's surprise visit. I followed the major's jeep into the entrance road and up to the chain-link and concertina wire that surrounded the compound.

"Halt!" Who goes there?" Bell harshly whispered.

I thought for sure he was putting on some kind of act for the major.

"Captain, is that you?" he whispered again.

"Who the hell did you expect?" I yelled, "the tooth fairy?"

"Quiet, captain! Get down! There's a sniper out there!" Bell whispered again, as a loud crack echoed in the hills.

He wasn't kidding! Some bastard was out there shooting at the 764th! The major, Bell and I got in our best "Camp Bullis crouch" and ran quickly into the breezeway. Hewitt, Dink, J.B. and Snake were already huddled there with their flak jackets on and M-16s loaded and ready. The almost full moon practically lit the whole compound, but the breezeway eaves left us in total darkness. We could look around the corner in the direction of the sniper fire.

"Issue the captain and major some equipment," ordered Bell.

"The major can have mine," said Snake, taking off his flak jacket. "I won't be needing it. I had a spiritual experience this afternoon. I was sitting on this sand dune when I was lifted up and—"

"What the hell is this guy taking?" asked the major.

"Nothing, sir," I replied. "He's very religious!"

"When did this shit start," I asked Bell.

"Just a little while ago, captain," said Bell, as another shot rang out. "I called for a chopper."

"I think I saw something run across that open patch of ground just outside the perimeter," J.B. said nervously.

By now, everybody's imagination was getting the better of them. Hewitt took all of this in stride. This was nothing for him and he assured us we had nothing to worry about as long as we stayed in the compound.

"No Gook in his right mind is going to come close to us. They're scared shitless of these dogs!" Tom assured us.

"I'm the ranking officer here!" proclaimed the major. "You'll take orders from me! Wait here. I'm going to work my way down to the end of the hospital to get a better look. Cover me!"

The major began inching his way down the side of the hospital covered by the shadows of the hospital eaves.

"Who the fuck does he think he is, Clint Eastwood?" Dinky whispered.

"Yeah!" whispered J.B., "The Gook, the Bad and the Ugly!"

"Let the SOB go," said Bell, "maybe he'll get shot!"

"There's no way this sniper is going to shoot anything unless he has a target," I said. "These dogs are protected on three sides by concrete walls."

By now, the major had almost made it to the end of the hospital. He was standing in the mud puddle that was always present below the air conditioner that stuck out of the surgery. All of a sudden, there was a loud *crackle, crackle* – the unmistakable sounds of electricity.

"God damn it, Kubisz! Get this air conditioner grounded!"

The major's whispered scream was all we needed to send all of us into fits of laughter to the point of tears. Bell was rolling around on the ground holding his side. Snot was coming out of Snake's nose and tears were rolling down Dink's cheeks. If it wasn't for the helicopter showing up, we would have laughed all night. The chopper scanned the area with its search lights, but no shots were exchanged and everything remained quiet.

We never did find the sniper, or find out whether it was the enemy or some guy just clowning around. The major survived his minor electrocution, but never again showed his face after hours at the 764th.

Tom tries to show me that Paper still has it!

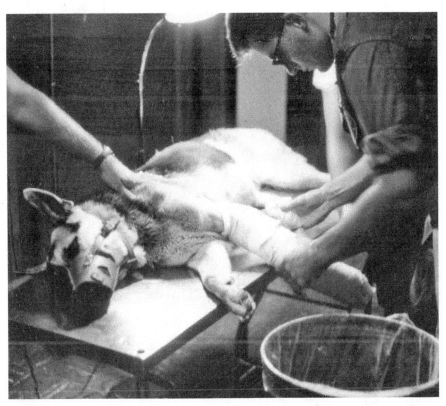

Examining Paper's wound after six weeks. Every day Paper presented a new challenge to me and the 764th!

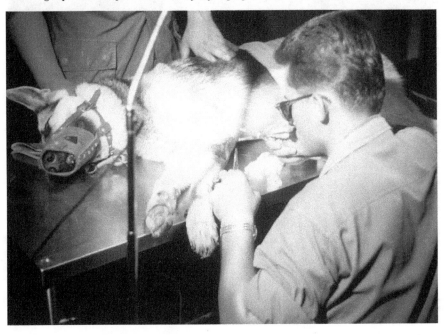

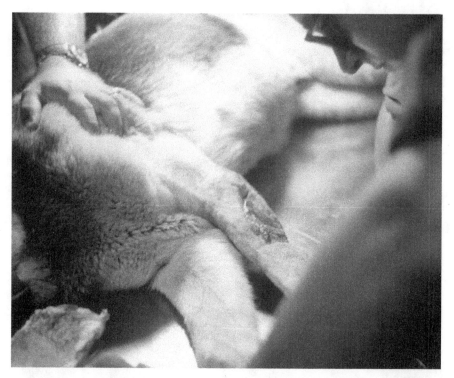

After six weeks there wasn't any skin left for me to cover Paper's wound.

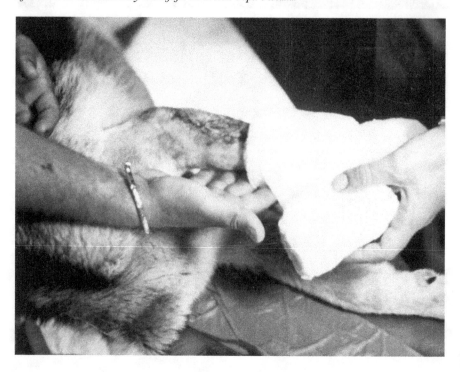

XIII.

The Skin Graft

IT WAS NOW THE FIFTH WEEK. Paper was again presented to the treatment room and I made the announcement that we would lose his cast. No one ever knew what my next move would be. Most of the time, I didn't know what I was going to do next. I was working on my old ESP. Paper seemed to know. That morning he was especially eager as he trotted down the hallway. The increased exercise had strengthened his muscles to the point where he easily threw his heavy cast around like it was part of him. I removed the tape, the cast, and the pads over the wound. I told Hewitt to put Paper down and let him go.

Hewitt placed Paper on the floor. Almost without thinking, Paper tried out his new leg. Most of my other patients after a cast removal were reluctant to use their leg. Paper wasn't going to baby it and used it immediately. He placed his weight directly on it, flexing and extending his paw like an athlete doing his warm-up exercises. Everything seemed to work, but when he moved forward and all the weight shifted to the injured leg, he still limped severely.

The hole in his leg that two hands couldn't cover had been reduced to the size of my large palm. The granulation tissue had extended to the surface of the hole and was even with the rest of the surrounding skin. This remained the primary problem. We had exhausted all available skin in the area and had stretched it to the max. But I put all my doubts aside for the moment and shared the joy that everyone was feeling and just watched Paper walk around without his cast. He would need a lot of exercises to regain all the use of his muscles.

"You know what I'd like to do, captain?" Hewitt asked. I'd like to take Paper swimming. He used to love to swim."

"I can't see anything wrong with that," I agreed. "Maybe the salt water will have some beneficial effect on the granulation tissue."

Every day, after work was finished, we'd all pile into the three-quarter ton truck and head for the beach. Paper really did love to swim. He seemed inexhaustible as he would swim for hours. We made beach therapy a part of all injured dogs' physical therapy. This was terrific in building them up and it was a good excuse to get out to the beach anytime we felt like it.

When I think of the pleasant memories of Vietnam, I recall one bright, sunny day at the beach. I was standing on the white sand shore, the cloudless blue sky was reflecting off the blue-green ocean. In the distance, Hewitt and Paper were running towards me. As they got closer and closer, I could see Tom smiling and Paper looked like he was smiling too.

"What do you think of our miracle dog now, Captain K?" Hewitt yelled, coming to a stop in front of me. "This 101st Scout Dog is ready for duty!"

I can still picture that moment like it was yesterday... as clear as looking through a time window; and when I do, I smile. And I can recall the bad memory of having to tell Hewitt later that same day, that Paper wouldn't be going back to the war; the best I could hope for was reassignment to Okinawa.

"No, captain! NO!! We've got to get back. They need us!" Hewitt urged.

I had almost hoped that Tom wanted an early ticket out of 'Nam, but he wasn't that kind of a guy. He knew that men's lives depended on both of them. Every day that they were at Cam Ranh, a lot of men were out of their best insurance policy. Every day without Tom and Paper on patrol meant someone would probably die. All scout dogs were in short supply and Paper wouldn't be easy to replace.

"What can I tell you, Hewitt?" I asked. That hole in Paper's leg is going to be there for months. It will eventually fill in with scar tissue, but that's not much of an improvement. He can still be used to train other dogs."

"There's got to be something else. We've come too far now. Look what you've done!" Hewitt bolstered.

We both stood back for a moment not saying anything and looking at Paper. He looked back with that same concern that we had. Neither of us could look the other in the eye.

"What about a skin graft?" Tom asked. "Don't they do skin grafts on dogs, like they do people?"

I had only read about skin grafts in school. I never even saw one performed and they didn't teach us much about them. I knew that they rarely worked on dogs and it required some expertise and a lot of time. The constant flexion of this area would also pose a problem with any graft.

"OK Tom," I said. "Paper has beaten all the odds, but it's not something I can do. I don't even know if it's possible. I'll go out to the Air Force Hospital and see if I can find someone qualified in doing grafts."

"That's all I ask, Doctor J," Tom sighed. "We can't give up yet!"

I drove through the main gate of the Air Force Hospital and exchanged salutes with the M.P. guard. I was already pretty familiar with the layout of this large hospital and proceeded to the main building for surgery. I asked the desk sergeant about seeing a surgeon who could do skin grafts.

"You want Doctor Bob," he confidently answered. "Doctor Bob Eilert, he's the best; down the hall in the orthopedic section, captain."

I could already see the sign down the hall, "Orthopedics." Skin grafts come under the department of orthopedics because a lot of the techniques and procedures are similar to working with bones, except the skin is flexible. As I walked into the first room, I was confronted by a young guy in hospital scrubs. I figured he was some kind of hospital orderly. He didn't look like he had started shaving yet.

"Can you tell me where I can find Dr. Bob Eilert, my man?" I asked him.

"You found him, Jack!" he replied.

"You're Dr. Bob?" I asked, surprised.

"Yes I am," he answered. Most people are surprised at first. They expect this gray-haired old man with a pot belly."

"I know what you mean," I commented. "Everyone pictures veterinarians as short, fat, balding men with thick glasses."

We exchanged introductions and shook hands. Bob had graduated from Johns Hopkins. He had two years of residency and specialized in orthopedic surgery. He graduated the bottom of his class in age, and the top scholastically – a boy genius. We seemed to get along right from the start and saw the Army and Vietnam with the same eyes. I told him about Paper as best I could, and a few other cases while I was at it. I always tried to pump as much info. as possible when I found someone like this. I was never a person to keep my mouth shut, but when I find someone of this intelligence, I'm all ears. I told Bob about the special relationship between Hewitt and Paper. I also described the granulation tissue and the problem of returning a dog to duty if there was any excessive scar tissue.

"Sounds interesting," he said. "I never worked on a dog before. Tomorrow, I have the day off. Maybe I could get over to take a look see?"

I told him if there was any chance, I would send someone to pick him up at whatever time he wanted. He told me that wouldn't be necessary. I had convinced him to come out and he would be there at 9AM sharp.

"Don't you mean 0900 hours?" I joked.

"Up your 0900!" he laughed.

I always liked doctors like this guy – the kind that shoots from the hip. So many of them graduate and end up in a merry-go-round of lab tests and procedures, never giving you a direct answer and wearing their degree like lifers wore their medals, placing themselves above "ordinary" people and losing their ability to communicate with anybody. Most of these types have the bedside manner of a leech and rely on two-foot long words to impress their patients. Dr. Bob didn't need any approval from his superiors, or any Army formal requisition to lend his expertise. He would do whatever he could, to the best of his ability, and I knew he would be there on time – even for a dog named "Paper"!

I returned to the 764th with the news that I had found the skin graft specialist we were looking for. Hewitt was happy to hear that we had one last chance, but I told him that this Dr. Bob didn't paint any pretty pictures and he had never worked on a dog.

"Wait 'til you see this guy, Tom. He looks like your younger brother, but he's some kind of boy genius. I just hope he says graft is possible."

We all anxiously awaited the arrival of Dr. Bob the next morning. I had everybody hopping to clean up the hospital. Someone even found some wax for our tile floors. The place looked and smelled great. I didn't want Dr. Bob to think that vet medicine was still in the Stone Age. He was used to the best facilities in the world and we might not be up to his standards, but at least we were going to be clean.

"Thar she blows!" J.B. yelled from the top of the hospital's roof.

The roof was the vantage point we used to view the surrounding area. If the major or colonel was expected, someone took the lookout position in the "crow's nest," on top of the hospital. We couldn't be expected to look Army and be in the required uniform, or busy all the time. So, when the lookout yelled "Thar she blows", we all knew someone was coming and to man our "battle stations," J.B. was the usual person on the roof, taking in his sounds and getting some rays. He would strain his eyes looking for the first telltale signs of dust that would signal an approaching vehicle. I had all the men fall out at the gate, stand at attention and give their best salute. Dr. Bob was right on time.

"Cut the bullshit!" Dr. Bob laughed, as he got out of his jeep.

I shook his hand and thanked him for making time to see Paper. I introduced him to the Dirty Half Dozen.

"What else am I going to do on my day off?" he asked. "See the sites of Cam Ranh Bay?" he laughed.

I told Hewitt to bring Paper from the kennel and I gave Dr. Bob the ten cent tour of the hospital. In X-ray, I showed him four or five cases, including Paper's, that were hospitalized at that time. I felt somewhat insecure or inadequate with my procedures in the presence of this expert. He quietly reviewed all the cases: a fractured femur, a fractured tibia, a fractured humerus and Paper's severely fractured radius and ulna. Most of them had stainless steel pins inserted into their bones. Dr. Bob studied each case in complete silence, not making any comments or judgments.

"What do you think?" I finally asked. "Pretty medieval, huh?"

"On the contrary," Bob reassured, "I'm impressed. I didn't realize that veterinary medicine had come so far. To tell the truth, I wouldn't have done any of these cases differently. I'm also impressed with your use of intramedullary pins. I've always favored them over plates and screws."

I think everyone needs an ego boost, once in a while, like I got that morning. Here was a man that I already respected and who had a lot of experience not available to me. I came fresh out of vet school with very little practical experience and I was still unsure of a lot of things that I was attempting. I thought we had done everything possible with Paper, but I always felt we could have done more. Hewitt was already in the exam room across the hall, nervously listening to our discussion over Paper's radiographs. I was showing over a dozen to Dr. Bob that detailed the progression of Paper's fracture.

"This is incredible healing in a short amount of time!" Dr. Bob remarked. "How the hell can this dog walk on it after six weeks? Let me get a good look at this wonder dog!"

Bob knew that Hewitt was listening to every word and I think he wanted for Hewitt to hear his comments. We entered the exam room together. Paper gave a low, warning growl as he noticed a new face.

"That's OK boy. He's going to help you. Just relax," Hewitt consoled.

"Go ahead, Bob," I urged. "You can trust this dog with your life!"

"As long as he doesn't take my life!" Dr. Bob quipped. "I may be the one who needs the skin graft."

Cautiously at first, he approached Paper and carefully examined the area of the proposed skin graft. He studied it, again in silence, and now I knew how the rest of the men felt when they waited for my decision on something they had no knowledge of. It was my turn to be the nervous observer. He stared at the wound thoughtfully, pushing it from side to side. Then, he gave a little squeeze. Hewitt looked nervously at me and I looked back and shrugged my shoulders.

"I don't see why we can't do Paper just like we do people," Bob finally said. "The healing is truly remarkable and you're at the perfect stage for a graft."

Hewitt and I exchanged smiles and thumbs up.

"When can we do it?" I asked.

"How about right now?" Dr. Bob returned.

We made the necessary preparations. Dr. Bob checked our available equipment, gas machine, instruments, suture material and so on. This was going to be the kind of surgery they did downtown. It was a rare chance to do surgery with an expert in his field. The surgery would require complete sterility; cap, gown and masks. Everyone prepared like bees in a hive. Hewitt gave Paper his usual pre-surgery pep talk like a coach giving instructions before the big game.

"I don't suppose you have a dermatone?" Dr. Bob asked.
"No, I'm sorry," I said. "But we traded about a half a dozen cables to the Air Force – made out like bandits!" I joked.

"That's alright," he sighed, "I need practice doing it the old fashioned way."

Dr. Bob brought out the best in all of us. We wanted to measure up to the standards to which he was accustomed. Paper was sedated and placed on the gas machine. Paper and Hewitt had been through the routine a dozen times. The flank area just above the rear leg was shaved and surgically prepped. We would remove the four inch piece of skin necessary for the graft from this area because it provided a lot of loose skin that could be easily removed. The graft site below the elbow was prepared.

"Careful prepping that granulation tissue!" Bob ordered Dinky.

"You have to be very careful with it to avoid bleeding. Any blood under the graft and it won't take."

The areas of surgery were draped and ready. I would assist Dr. Bob on his right; Dow would be across the table; Bell was on gas; Snake and J.B. stood their distance in the hallway, unmasked and without gowns. Bob quickly picked up a scalpel and removed the four inch square piece of skin from the flank. The large hole that was left was barely bleeding.

"Why don't you suture that flank incision, John, while I prepare this piece of skin," Bob suggested.

He stepped away from the surgery table with the flap of skin and began doing something with it using a scalpel. He placed it on a sterile towel on the instrument tray and started peeling the layers of epidermis away.

"What are you doing?" I asked as I began to suture the flank incision.

"I have to reduce the thickness of this skin down to tissue-paper thinness. The thinner it is, the better the chances of success," he answered.

"Oh, I see," I said, but I really didn't. "That's what a dermatone does?"

"Right," he answered. "But if you do this right, this is just as good, maybe better, if you're patient."

And patient is what Dr. Bob was. It took over 30 minutes, but when he was finished, there was a piece of skin three inches by four inches that was practically transparent. There wasn't as much as a nick in the entire piece. He held it up to the light.

"Not bad, huh?" he asked.

"Right on!" remarked Bell.

"Unbelievable!" was my two cents.

"Not bad on the flank incision, Dr. J," Bob commented.

"Oh, sure! Throw the poor Polish kid a bone," I said.

Dr. Bob continued the operation by placing the thin skin sample over the raw granulation tissue. He began placing one stitch at a time around the graft in a circle, leaving the ends long. One after another, he proceeded to tack down the graft until there were dozens of stitches with long ends like the spokes of a bicycle wheel. We silently observed.

"One more ought to do it," he said. "Now, I need a ball of cotton soaked in glycerin to put in the middle and begin the second part of the operation."

When the cotton was in place, he began tying the long ends of the suture material over the top of the cotton to hold it in place until it looked like a spider's web. He was almost finished when an unexpected visitor came into the surgery.

"What the hell's going on and who the hell is this?"

The obnoxious sound of the major's voice broke the tranquil intensity of the surgical theatre.

"Why are you still screwing around with that damn dog?" he snarled. "I think he's dead meat and doesn't know it!"

"This 'Damn Dog', major, has an excellent chance of making it," Bob responded.

"And what makes you an expert?" sneered the major.

Dr. Bob started spouting off his credentials and then I jumped in with a few more and by the time we were finished, Kraft had little to say.

"Yeah, yeah! You're a specialist in people, but you've never worked on a dog. I know dogs! Anyway, I'm not out here for that. I just came by to inform you in person, Captain Kubisz, that the new C.O. for the 176th has arrived and you are to report to him as soon as possible," he said, rolling his eyes back and sneering. "I wanted to bring you to him myself, but I see you're busy."

"Major!" Dr. Bob interrupted. "I'm doing a very important surgery here and if you're not sterile, please leave the room!"

"Report to the new colonel ASAP!" Kraft concluded smirking and then waddling out in a huff.

"That bastard is sterile, alright," I said. "The Army put his balls in formaldehyde when he reached major!"

"It's guys like him that make the military suck," Dr. Bob concurred. "They're looking for their next medal or promotion. This dog is more deserving of a medal – at least a Purple Heart."

"The Army has a policy of no medals for dogs, for whatever reasons," I said.

"If they gave medals, Paper would have a collar full."

"There's a lot of guys out there right now that would gladly give Paper a medal," Hewitt continued. "He saved their asses a hundred times and they're all waiting for our return."

Hewitt went on to tell how he loved to report to a new unit's C.O. Most of these guys never saw a war dog in action. Most of them expected some kind of military watch dog. After seeing what these dogs were actually capable of doing, scout dogs quickly became the top priority on the want lists for all combat units.

The skin graft was finally completed and Paper was doing fine.

"We need some way to immobilize this entire leg," Dr. Bob announced.

"Hewitt, you still have Paper's old cast. Why don't you see if it's what Dr. Bob needs?" I asked.

Again, the old reliable cast was perfect for the job. We applied the cast like we had done dozens of times and gave Paper an injection of antibiotics to prevent any possibilities of a new infection.

"He's going to have to remain very quiet. No exercise or activity for one week. This is to insure fixation. We have to get at least half the graft to take. I'll be back in one week," Dr. Bob finished.

Hewitt and the rest of us thanked Dr. Eilert for his time and consideration. Hewitt returned Paper to his run and stayed with him again until Paper had recovered from his anesthetic. When everything was secured, I headed for the 176th and the confrontation with the new colonel.

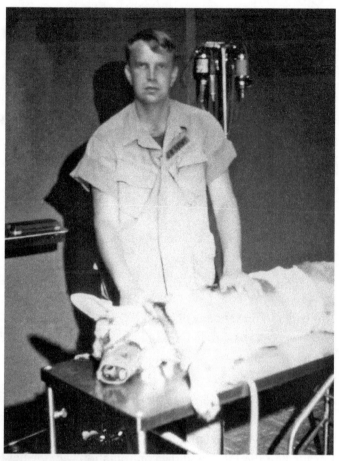

Above: This picture was taken immediately after the intensive skin graft surgery. The procedure lasted three-hours. Everyone could see the stress in Tom's eyes after the prolonged skin graft.

Left: Paper was soon up and about again.

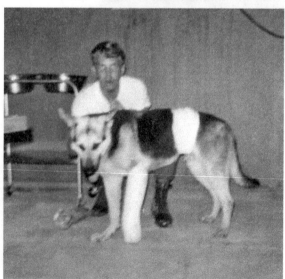

XIV.

Colonel SOB and the IG's SOP

THE 176TH VETERINARY DETACHMENT was in a long quonset building among all the other quonset huts in the main Army base at Cam Ranh Bay. The forward section contained a dozen desks for the company clerks and for the veterinary captains that were directly assigned to them. They all had food inspecting duties. The C.O.'s office (the colonel) was in the back of the building. I pulled my jeep up to the front of the office area. As I entered the building I could immediately feel the tension that previously was never there. The normally cheerful E.M.s were uptight and in complete uniform attire with shined boots, sporting fresh cut, short hair. I looked at the clerk who was their version of our J.B., but now he looked G.I. straight.

"Nice hair cut!" I commented.

He just rolled his eyes back and shook his head negatively.

"This new colonel is a real mother!" he quietly announced. "Watch yourself, captain!"

I preceded the length of the double-rowed desks to the last one. The major who was sitting behind his desk in front of the colonel's office looked up at me and smiled.

"I'll tell Colonel Gallagher you're here. He can't wait to see you!" Major Kraft sneered coldly.

It looked like the old days of Colonel LaMarr were over. LaMarr was harmless enough. He just put in his time, not making waves, waiting for retirement. Now he was Stateside and his new replacement was regular Army, bucking for full-bird colonel. He had done a pretty good job of making everyone else jump. Now it was my turn.

"Go right in, Captain Kubisz," the major urged, with a smirk on his already obnoxious face.

"Captain Kubisz, reporting as ordered, sir!" I snapped to attention and saluted.

The colonel gave a half-ass return salute from the seated position and told me to stand at ease – not to have a seat, or shake my hand, or offer an introduction but to just stand at ease.

This was one of those clowns who thought he was something special because he had survived all the bullshit and was now a genuine lieutenant colonel. Again, I was asking myself why anyone would trade their humanity for this horse manure. You would need a proctologist to find this guy's diploma. I stood at my best parade rest! His fatigues were starched, his hair short and his boots shined to perfection.

"Captain," he began slowly, "you're some kind of legend in the Veterinary Corps, almost to the point of being notorious."

"I can assure you, sir, that most of the stories you've heard are greatly exaggerated," I mistakenly interrupted. The ranks above captain were major, indicated by a gold leaf on their lapel; lieutenant colonel, indicated by a silver leaf; and colonel, indicated by an eagle (hence, full-bird).

"Hold it right there, captain!" he ordered. "Don't interrupt me again! I've seen a lot of guys with your bullshit before, and you'll just stand there until I have finished! Anyway, things are going to change around here. The 764th isn't going to be operating much longer. It will eventually be placed under my command, the 176th. And, this whole process will be greatly accelerated after the IG is finished with your outfit. Do you even know what an IG is, captain?"

I remained standing there at parade rest and shook my head widely from side to side.

"I didn't think so," he continued. "The IG is a general inspection that brings fear to all Company Commanders, including me. I'm quite sure that when they're done with your outfit of misfits and degenerates, they'll recommend immediate annexation of your unit into mine," he gloated.

"They're also going to eliminate all the deadwood around there. The major tells me you've had one dog and handler tied up for six weeks! This kind of nonsense is going to stop. Now, I want you to return to that unit of yours and try to get it in some kind of shape so that you are not too much of an embarrassment to the Veterinary Corps. The IG on the 764th is in two weeks. That is all!" His eyes looked directly in front of him at the desk top.

I didn't give a rat's ass about this asshole's opinion of me or my unit. We didn't answer to anyone except each other. But when he started stepping on the toes of Tom and Paper, I started a slow burn. What the hell did this nincompoop know about what we had been through? Now, this jerk is going to tell me what he's going to do with my patients? If you're ever in a fight, you'd better make sure I'm on your side! I slowly came back to attention and put my hand up in a salute. I knew he had to return it, even if he didn't want to. I stood there for two or three minutes until he eventually looked up and weakly returned my salute. Then I did my best about face and walked out. The major could hear everything through the thin walls and be grinning ear to ear when I passed his desk.

"You finally have someone to kiss up to!" I bravely snapped removing the smile from his face.

I walked too quickly for the major to respond, down the aisle of desks with everyone in the office watching me. I got into my jeep and took off, throwing sand with my tires. Now I had two Major Krafts to deal with. But this new one was a rank higher and more dangerous. They were determined to destroy the 764th and everyone in it. It really burned their asses that I was under the direct command of the general in Saigon. My only advantage was that the Army didn't ever do anything quickly and they needed a pretty good reason to change anything. If I could play their game and beat them, I could slow the whole process even more. I returned to the 764th, still boiling. I called a meeting of everyone in the office and informed them of this new colonel and his little speech.

"I am determined to show this jack-off, colonel SOB, that it doesn't take any brains to play Army!" I announced. "Granny, do you know anything about an IG?"

"I've been through a few, captain, "he replied. "They're not easy, but we can get ready in two weeks if we all work hard!"

"Great!" I replied. "I knew you would come in handy someday. I'm putting Porter in charge of this whole operation. You all will do exactly like he orders. And stop your groaning! If you guys don't want your asses in the front office of the 176th and taking orders from that jerk-face colonel, we'd better pass this IG with flying colors!"

"Can they do anything about Paper?" Hewitt asked.

"I doubt it. But if that skin graft fails, I don't know how much time he'll have left," I warned.

Everybody got in high gear and started working immediately under Porter's instruction. Preparing for the IG helped the week pass quickly, but all of us worried about Paper – and all Paper could do was sit in his cage and wait. He couldn't go to the beach for his daily swim; he couldn't play with Sherman or even Hewitt. He had to patiently sit in his cage and watch the activities around him. He must have wondered what the hell got into all of us. While he sat in his run all day, we were running around like chickens with their heads cut off. Again, Paper could have destroyed all the work we had meticulously performed. He certainly had the strength now to do so. But again, he seemed to understand and accept his week's sentence of complete confinement. By the end of the week, our anxiety had peaked and all of us nervously waited for Dr. Bob's arrival. Paper was as anxious as any of us when he entered the exam room with Hewitt.

"Paper followed your orders, Dr. Bob," Hewitt proudly proclaimed.

"He didn't once even look at his leg."

We slowly unwrapped the cast and began removing the layers of gauze from around the cotton padded graft. The sutures holding the cotton in place were removed. The grafted area was now visible. We all huddled around like a football team. None of us, except Dr. Bob, knew whether it was a success or failure. To me, it looked gray and lifeless. Again, Dr. Bob studied it carefully, in silence.

"The graft a complete success," he calmly announced.

There was a general sigh of relief. No cheering or celebrating this time, more of an answer to a prayer. Hewitt gave Paper a big hug and Paper wagged his tail in appreciation. We would still have to protect the graft for another week before removing all the bandages and stitches completely. You could feel the drama in the room begin to grow. Every one of us was filled with pride and enthusiasm. A miracle had taken place; Paper's chances of returning to duty took a giant step forward.

"Thanks for everything, Dr. Bob," I said. "I wish I had better words. But you know what it means to us."

"I think I have some idea. Glad to be of assistance. Take good care of him, Tom," Dr. Bob said.

"Don't worry, Dr. Bob. He's my brother!" Hewitt assured.

Dr. Eilert left and we never saw him again. He was short (not a long time left in the country) and returned to the States a couple of weeks later. He would never know Paper's fate, but it was his expertise that was the final stage in Paper's treatment.

In a few days, I removed all of the remaining stitches and, for the first time in days, we hit the beaches. The salt water again seemed to speed the healing. Hair was already growing in the area of the graft and the flank incision healed like a charm.

While Paper enjoyed his new found freedom, the troops were busy with their preparations for the approaching IG. Porter even found some Army manual for preparing for an IG. Our number one spy, Dusty, who was now confined to the front office of the 176th, would relate any information he could that would help our efforts. He would do what he could to sabotage or slow down their progress.

One of the biggest problems confronting us was our unit's TOE (Table of Organization and Equipment). A few things were missing, but we had tons of shit we weren't supposed to have. We had bartered, stolen and traded all kinds of stuff that accumulated quickly in the last eight months. What were we supposed to do with all of it now? Throw it on the scrap heap? Taylor solved the problem for us. The 981st M.P.s were facing their IG the day after ours and the unit was equally out of balance with their TOE. We would move all the unauthorized junk that didn't belong from the 764th to the 981st. Then the following day, we would move it back along with the 981st stuff. The equipment we were missing, we would borrow, so to speak, from wherever we could find it.

While we had the additional week of preparing for this stupid IG, all the other work, including the war wounded, had to be continued. One morning I had orthopedic surgery on one of the sentry dogs that had broken a femur on patrol the night before. With a lot of orthopedic surgery, you never know what complications you'll run into, and sometimes there's a lot of sweating and swearing. But I still enjoyed orthopedics. I guess it was like playing with Tinker Toys or Erector Sets when I was a kid. Orthopedics requires imagination and you're never quite sure what you'll run into until you get started – hammer here, drill there.

As I cussed and fussed over the new case, I felt the presence of someone else at the edge of the room and looked to see the new colonel – Gallagher.

"And what can I do for you, colonel?" I abruptly asked.

He didn't say a word, just turned around and left. I don't know how long he was standing there observing. Everybody presented the one finger salute when he left. I'm very sure the 764th left him quite speechless. He expected to find this run-down garbage dump of an Army unit after he heard all the wild stories that were floating around about us. We might have had a reputation bordering on notorious as far as the Army goes, but as far as an animal hospital, you would have to go far to find a better one.

There were three things that I insisted on: that the dogs received the best medical and surgical attention possible; that when our part was complete to the best of our abilities, the hospital and kennels were always immaculate and spotless; and that Snake kept his grass off the 764th grounds.

With six people working full time, the hospital was always a thing of beauty. When I ran out of things to clean and polish, I'd ask for volunteers to go across the bay and dig up plants and palm trees to make the outside area look good. Dow sent a request home for some seeds and before long we had marigolds, pansies, and tomatoes growing in the back of the hospital.

Preparations continued for the IG. We tried to cover all avenues, no matter how insignificant. Everyone was ordered to have at least one set of fatigues washed and starched at the base laundry, just like the upper brass. Boots were to be spit-shined and hair was to be G.I. short. Bell went somewhat overboard and had his head shaved; he was followed by J.B. I even had the dogs wormed early. This was a routine requirement, and some might ask how in the hell did it help? The dogs were all given an organic phosphate medication monthly to help combat hookworms. The medication passed in their stools almost unchanged and any flies feeding on it also died. This procedure wiped out all the flies in the area.

Porter was a great help in the paper end of the IG. He would go over and over every requirement and regulation the Army had. Granny accounted for all of the SOP, TOE and every other three-letter abbreviation the Army had to offer. For the first time, I had given him the authority that he wanted and he had the men jumpin' as if I had made him general. I was in complete agreement with everything he asked them to do because I knew absolutely nothing about the requirements of an IG. I did, however, manage to squeeze my size 12 feet into some regulation boots. I sat right with the other guys shining them.

"I can't believe you're going to wear boots, Captain K," remarked Bell. "I've never seen you in boots."

"These boots are made for the IG only," I responded, which sent Bell into an immediate chorus of Nancy Sinatra's old song:

These boots are made for the IG,
And that's just what they'll do
We're going to kick their asses
From Cam Ranh to Pleiku!

"Please, Ding, spare us!" yelled J.B. as he turned the volume up on the Stones. "I can't get no — !"

We worked continuously up to the morning of the IG. We were up at the crack of dawn and everyone made one final check of everyone else. J.B. took his position in the crow's nest. It was about 8 AM.

"Here they come!" yelled J.B. "It looks like a huge damn parade. There must be seven or eight vehicles!"

Everyone got in their accustomed battle stations and nervously awaited the inquisition. Porter greeted them at the gate and almost immediately one of them was writing on his clipboard. They hardly said a word. Every inch of the 764th was scrutinized, along with every man and his position. Any minute I expected them to ask us to drop our pants for a short-arm inspection. Everything they challenged, Porter countered. I knew we were looking good.

Hewitt observed everything from the confines of the 981st M.P.s, about 50 feet away. We all sweated that they would finish early and start their inspection of the 981st insuring that both units would go down the drain. Taylor and Tom started staging some attack training to give them second thoughts about even getting close to their space.

The inspectors completed every aspect of their IG with a minimal amount of questions or comments. What appeared to be their leader, looked at me and gave me the thumbs up. We not only passed, but we also got the highest rating of any unit at Cam Ranh, easily surpassing the 176 Vet Detachment. We would never take a backseat to them again. The general himself came from Saigon to the 764th to commend us on the fine job that we were doing. He was already aware of the efforts of the 176 to annex my unit but assured me privately that as long as I was the C.O., the 764th would stay independent.

"You know," the general stated, "I'll make you a field promotion to major if you extend another six months, Captain K!"

The thought alone sent cold chills down my back.

"General, sir," I said slowly, "with all due respect, I wouldn't extend for another six minutes!"

"I know," he sighed reluctantly, "the Army's lost another good one! Carry on!" We didn't exchange salutes. He reached out and shook my hand. But at least for now, the fate of the 764th was secured and Hewitt wouldn't have to worry about Paper. There would be no limits placed on his recovery. The 764th could be even bolder than they were before. We had beaten them again at their own game. We had successfully pulled off the impossible again and it was time to party. Dinky was in charge of commandeering a case of ribs and a case of steaks from cold storage. Hewitt, Ding and I headed across the bay to the village of Bon Nhoi to secure some crab and lobster for the celebration. While we were there, we bought the biggest lobster any of us had ever seen. It weighed 25 pounds! We returned late in the afternoon and were met at the gate by J.B. He looked in the back of the three-quarter ton and saw the lobster.

"Damn!" he said. "These roaches are getting out of hand!"

It was time to relax and enjoy our victory. The team's effort had won the game. If there was one thing we were better at than working together, it was playing together. We could be like kids getting out of school for summer vacation. Even Paper and Sherman would get into the act. A little note for the reader: a 25 pound lobster tastes as good as a small one! I announced at the party that I was presenting Porter with the Army's Commendation Medal for his efforts in the IG. The next morning found everyone very hung-over and cross-eyed, to say the least. After morning sick call, I ordered everyone to fall out by the statue of Snoopy, including Hewitt, Paper, and Sherman. J.B. would capture the moment on film and provide some military music. While J.B. played *Hail to the Chief*, I ordered Specialist 6 Porter front and center.

"By direction of the Secretary of the Army," I began, "the Army Commendation Medal is presented to Specialist 6, Francis Ulysses Porter of the United States Army Veterinary Corps, who distinguished himself by exceptionally meritorious service in support of military operations against communist aggression in the Republic of South Vietnam. He astutely surmounted extremely adverse conditions to obtain consistently superior results. Through diligence and determination, he invariably accomplished every task with dispatch and efficiency. His wide acclaim has inspired others to strive for maximum achievement. Selflessly working long and arduous hours, he had contributed significantly to the success of the allied effort. His commendable performance in helping the 764th Medical Detachment pas their IG was in keeping with the finest traditions of military service and reflects distinct credit upon himself and the Army."

I shook his hand and everyone saluted. Granny stood proudly as I pinned the medal on him.

"Good job, Ulysses!" said J.B.

Just about as soon as the ceremony broke up, Hewitt came over to me with Paper.

Left: Tom proudly poses Paper with the skin graft bandage off.

Below: Job well done by the 764th! Here I am pinning the Army Commendation Medal on Francis Porter (not real name). From the left is Richard Teagrass (not real name); Spec. 4 Francis Bell (real name); Spec. 5 David Dow (real name); Bowman (temporary replacement)real name but only a private. James B. Jones is taking the picture; real name and (I think) Private 1st Class. Snoopy in the background.

XV.

Paper's Test of Fire

"WE ARE READY, DOC, TO RETURN TO DUTY!" Tom announced. "I'm enjoying all the fun and games, but me and Paper have to get back."

I stared at him. How could anybody be in a hurry to get back to that hell-hole of a war? But I also knew that it had to be. They had some destiny to fulfill and it was only my will that kept them at Cam Ranh. Maybe if I kept them there long enough, the war would just end.

"You might think you're ready to return, but you two aren't the same combat veterans I saw eight weeks ago. You're both a couple of marshmallows," I jabbed. "I think we need at least a couple runs in simulated combat conditions before you get too cocky!"

For the first time, there was no doubt in my mind that not only would Paper survive, but he would eventually be returned to full-time active duty. We had overcome all the obstacles that, looking back, were unbelievable or even miraculous. Why did Hewitt want to jeopardize Paper's life again, and his own? Also for the first time, the urgency of Paper's recovery was behind us. I could finally talk to Hewitt about his life and his relationship with Paper. Before this time, I didn't want to get any closer to Hewitt and Paper than I already was. It was impossible not to like Tom, and not just because he was from Indiana. He had this wholesome farm boy appearance and attitude that no one could refuse. He became like the younger brother that I never had. Paper was my dog, as well as his. One evening in the kennels, I was alone with Tom and Paper and we just started talking.

"How did you and Paper ever get together?" I asked, "And, how did you ever become a scout dog handler, Tom?"

"Well, Doc," Hewitt started. "It's kind of a long story. I started out as a kid training horses on a farm outside of Muncie, Indiana. I knew I was headed for 'Nam, but I qualified for N.C.O. (Non Commissioned Officer) school. After two weeks, I couldn't picture myself as a sergeant in Vietnam, so I asked for a transfer. With my animal training background, they asked if I would like to try my hand at dog training. I actually started with a different dog and after a couple of days, the drill sergeant thought that Paper better suited my personality and super intelligence!" he laughed.

"Paper fit me, alright. We were perfect for each other from day one. We spent ten weeks alone on basic obedience training with Paper on a leash at all times. Then, another fourteen weeks with off-lead training, detecting booby traps, ambushes, mines, gun powder, tunnels and such."

"Where did Paper come from and how did he get his name?" I inquired.

"I can only guess about his name, captain," Hewitt said.

"He was born about six weeks before Christmas and maybe he was a Christmas present and he liked to play with paper. He was actually a registered AKC German Shepherd who could have been a show dog except for one bum foot."

"What bum foot?" I asked. "I thought I knew this dog top to bottom in the last eight weeks."

"You can hardly notice it, but it's kind of like a slightly clubbed foot on his rear paw. If a judge in the show ring saw it, he would disqualify him, so the original owners donated Paper to the Army," Hewitt remarked.

"How does this airborne thing work?" I asked. "I know he's able to jump out of planes with you, but how does he do it?"

"He's attached to my waist with bungee cords and I jump, holding him in front of me. Then I drop him below me and open my chute!" he said confidently.

"Damn!" I said. "*Ripley's Believe It or Not!* So what the hell is the real story about Paper getting shot? I still can't see how you two got caught in a cross-fire between our guys and Charlie!"

"Easter morning," he started. "Easter morning is when he got shot, and we were supposed to be in a no-fire zone, no gooks were even supposed to be in the area. Earlier that morning we'd stopped to eat something and were sitting in some thick bamboo. You couldn't see ten feet in front of you. Paper went on alert in that crazy radar screen thing he does. There, walking up the trail, all alone, was a single gook. We wasted him. It was the closest

I'd ever see one shot before... he was practically on top of us before we shot him. We continued on patrol and kept seeing more and more signs of other gooks until we were in kind of a ravine and the gooks were scattered everywhere, and all hell broke loose! I'm not sure who shot Paper; maybe one of our own people!"

"Then," he continued, "we had to carry Paper for three days through the thickest shit I've ever been in, and pouring rain... like out of buckets! I'd carry him 'til I was exhausted, then someone else would carry him. We shared whatever food we had with him. I could see the bones of his leg sticking out and it never stopped bleeding. I knew from the smell on the second day, it was infected. But you know, Paper never once complained or cried. He's one tough dude!"

"He's tough alright," I concurred.

"The only thing I can tell for sure is that he was shot with an M-16, but the gooks had a lot of them too. He's just lucky to survive a hit from an M-16!"

"I know," Tom said. "I'm not blaming anyone, but I'm glad Paper made it, Doc. Thanks! I thought he was a goner."

"I'm glad he made it too, Tom, but Paper was helped by something or someone that needs most of the credit," I said, pointing up. "Why risk getting shot again? I can keep you both indefinitely now."

"We've got to get back. The 101st depends on us and I don't feel right being here while they're out there. Paper doesn't either. We've been from one end of the Ashau Valley to the other and I know that guys are dying because we aren't there," he warned.

I looked at Paper and Paper looked back at me as if to say, "Tom's right!"

"OK," I said. "My heart's not in it, but a man's got to do what a man's got to do! If you can show me that you two are able to take the rigors of patrol, and Paper's leg can hold up, then I'll send you back. But I'm going to make it a tough test to pass and I'm going to be there every minute, observing for the slightest reason not to send you back!"

"Right on, captain!" Hewitt cheered. "We'll show you!"

So, I organized the 764th to begin Paper's and Hewitt's retraining and reconditioning. They're going to start all over with the basics of on-lead obedience and work up to a day's march, through the boonies of Cam Ranh

Bay. I wasn't going to make it easy for them. The real thing would be a lot harder than anything I could dream up and a hell of a lot more dangerous.

Basic obedience was a breeze for Paper. I think he could have followed Hewitt's commands using mental telepathy. They were so "in tune with each other's vibes," like J.B. used to say.

Watching them perform, I thought about the quirk of fate that had brought them together. How, except for a slight defect, Paper could have been a pampered, prissy show dog. He could have lived a life of luxury and there would probably be a lot of little Papers running around by now. And maybe, Hewitt would be training horses for the rich and famous. But, for whatever reasons, they were together now and no one could picture them apart. Hewitt and Paper could easily pass this part of the test.

Next, we practiced simulated booby traps and ambushes. J.B., Dow, Bell, and Snake would hide along a simple trail in various enemy disguises. J.B. would be a sniper, or we would try three or four together in various postures. This experiment was a complete bust. Paper was either too smart for this façade or he thought we had gone completely mad. In every case, he would immediately run to the person hiding, knock them over and begin to lick them. The booby traps that we set up were knocked down and all the trip wires were sprung as if he wanted us to know that he wasn't playing our games.

"Give me some real gooks!" demanded Hewitt. "Then he'll play for keeps!"

"No!' I laughed. "You failed! Next test."

The next test was much more difficult for Paper and even more difficult for me to watch – the dreaded obstacle course! Dow and I stood outside the obstacle course enclosure one morning watching Hewitt put Paper through the course. The course was laid out to begin slow and easy and progress and build to the more demanding tests at the end. Paper started through the tunnel, through the low window, then through the water hazard, which was a breeze after all the beach training. Then, he proceeded up the ladder and across a narrow plank and down the ramp on the other side.

After this, Paper faced the most difficult sequence – one high hurdle and six barrels piled up in a pyramid. Paper's powerful hind legs propelled him over the high hurdles and he landed directly on his two front legs, giving his injured leg the first real test of its strength. You could see Paper's head pull back as he winced with pain, but he never made a sound and continued the course with a severe limp. I was just about to stop Hewitt from continuing, but it was too late. Paper gathered himself and pushed forward again and over the most difficult last jump. He hit the ground hard with his injured leg and again winced and limped even more severely.

"Damn!" Dow said. "That dog would go through hell for him!"

"I think he already has," I said. "Remember this dog, Dink, the next time you complain about a hang-nail. That's another thing 'Nam has taught me – never complain, and as far as that goes, never make excuses. Neither one ever does any good. We'd better take a look at that leg. I hope it's alright." Hewitt was congratulating Paper on completing the course successfully.

Paper was standing, holding his injured leg up.

"Let's take a look, Paper," I said, as I approached.

I held the leg in both hands and felt for any movement in the fracture. I could tell that the bones were okay but Paper was feeling some pain when I squeezed the leg. He still never made a sound and accepted any test I would perform.

"Is it OK, Doc?" Hewitt asked.

"I think so," I answered. "But I'm giving him three or four days off again."

Disappointed, Hewitt walked Paper back to his kennel and stayed with him a while. By the following morning, Paper acted as nothing happened and Hewitt was ready to test him again.

"NO!" I said firmly. "It's too risky!"

"How about the beach?" Hewitt urged. "The beach won't hurt."

I finally consented and Hewitt took Paper to the beach for the next two days, pushing Paper to the max in swimming and running in the sand. By the third day, he was running the obstacle course as well as any of the sentry dogs, maybe better!

"We're ready now, Doc!" Hewitt bragged. "About the only dog that could beat Paper is Rebel, and Rebel is just a dumb jock!"

I stood there just shaking my head and smiling. Hewitt was right. There wasn't another dog that could compare to Paper, ever with his injured leg. He was one of a kind. I would never see another like him. What tests did I have left that he couldn't pass?

"OK, OK!" I sighed, "I'm impressed. He's pretty good for the short haul, but how's he going to be running through jungles, rice paddies and up and down hills all day? How's the real thing? Tomorrow you and I are going on an all-day hike through the beautiful countryside of Cam Ranh Bay," I laughed. "Maybe after a ten of twenty mile hike in 120 degree heat, you'll both be singing a different tune!"

"You'll see, captain," Hewitt affirmed. "You'll be the first to cry, uncle. All you officers are wimps!" he laughed.

The next morning, we started out, Hewitt, Paper and I. I wasn't about to let Hewitt get the upper hand with this wimp officer! We started out quickly, but the morning was still cool and going easy. As the sun climbed in the sky, the temperature also climbed and soon we were cooking. But Paper did whatever Hewitt asked and didn't show any signs of slowing. The only one that was going to poop out first would be me, but I wasn't going to admit it.

"Had enough?" Hewitt taunted.

"Are you kidding? This is my usual morning stroll. Let's step up the pace!"

I valiantly struggled a couple more miles until I could see some fatigue in Hewitt and Paper.

"OK! You convinced me. Let's go back," I gasped.

"We did it, Paper, we did it! We're going back to the Screamin' Eagles!" Hewitt cheered.

Paper led the way back as he had done so many times as an off-lead scout dog. He had perfected this art like no other dog. Hewitt and I followed him about 50 yards behind. All of a sudden Paper stopped abruptly, sniffed the wind, and for the first time, I saw that crazy, radar screen way that Paper alerted. He lifted himself in the air on his hind legs and pivoted on them in both directions. Hewitt immediately dropped to the ground and motioned for Paper to get down. Tom looked back at me as I just stood there like some kind of an observer watching the two of them.

"Get down, captain!" Tom whispered. "Paper's alerted!"

"You've got to be kidding. No gook in his right mind is going to be out here!" I challenged.

"This is no false alarm. Paper doesn't make mistakes. And if you don't believe me, go ahead and try to move him. He'll rip your head off!" Tom warned.

Once before, Hewitt told me that when Paper was alerted, he only did so if there was danger and he couldn't be moved until the danger was discovered or removed. Sometimes in the boonies, he alerted and it took a long time to even find the problem – a concealed booby trap, a hidden stash of weapons or a lone gook. But whatever the problem, you had better find it or Paper would take your head off if you tried to move him. He was sure of his job and expertise.

"OK!" I whispered. "You convinced me." I got on the ground and rested on my elbows.

"Maybe he found that sniper that was shooting at us a couple of weeks ago. Now, what in the hell do we do? Our asses are out here with no weapons!"

I could tell from Hewitt's expression that he wasn't joking. This was the real thing, and I think both of us felt kind of shaky watching Paper frantically looking in one direction like a runner in the starting blocks.

"I'm moving up to see if I can see what he's looking at," Hewitt said softly.

I stayed put as Hewitt crawled to Paper. I was the veterinarian. Tom was a combat specialist. Hewitt moved up to Paper and motioned me to come forward.

"Whatever it is, it's over this small hill," Hewitt affirmed.

"There's nothing around here except sand and brush," I said.

We crawled together to the top of a low sand dune and looked into the valley below. There, just outside the fence and concertina wire was a lone Vietnamese, working on the fence. I recognized him as one of the regular old guys that did some menial jobs around the base. I slowly crawled to my feet, followed by Hewitt.

"It's OK, Paper," Hewitt reassured. "He's one of ours."

Paper relaxed immediately. Hewitt gave him a big pat on the head and told him that he was a good dog. Paper kept his eyes on the lone Vietnamese all the way down the hill and back to the 764th. I watched Tom and Paper, knowing that I had no more tests or excuses that I could use to keep them any longer. The time had come to say another goodbye.

XVI.

Another Goodbye

"Hey, captain, looks like your ass is draggin'," Dinky jabbed.

"Hell!" I responded, "Just getting warmed up! Let's go again!"

We sat in the breezeway of the hospital, out of the sun, where the wind cooled our sweat-soaked fatigues. Hewitt got Paper a bowl of water.

"They're going back," I announced quietly to Dinky.

He looked at me, then at Hewitt, almost in disbelief.

"You ain't goin' nowhere, grunt," Dink joked, "cause now I'm going to knock your head clean off!"

He grabbed Hewitt in a head lock and proceeded to playfully dance around the breezeway until Hewitt slipped loose.

"He's right, Dink," Hewitt said calmly, "we're going back."

Dinky opened the hospital door and then the office door.

"Get your asses out here! Doc says Hewitt and Paper are leaving us!" Dow yelled.

Everyone came out with that look of, "You've got to be kidding!"

No one said much. We all had to have time just to stand there and think about it. All of us knew this time would come and none of us had any good reasons to keep them any longer. J.B. made one last feeble attempt.

"Why don't you stay for my birthday party?" J.B. sounded. "It's only a couple of weeks away."

"No," said Hewitt. "You guys have done enough and it's time for me and Paper to hit the road."

"When they leavin'?" asked Snake.

"Tomorrow morning," was my cold reply.

My announcement hit hard and everyone was quiet. Bell broke the silence this time.

"I feel we should throw you two the biggest party the 764th has ever seen, but somehow I don't feel much like a party," Bell resigned.

"I don't think any of us are in the mood for a party," I agreed. "Let's get some chow and come back with a couple of cases of beer from the PX. We can spend the last night just sittin' around this joint. And I mean 'joint', like the hospital, Snake!" I laughed.

We returned to the hospital after mess and sat around the surgery room poppin' a few beers. It was air conditioned – something Paper and Hewitt wouldn't be seeing for a while. Paper had a little beer in his bowl. J.B., Dow, Bell, Snake, and even Granny pressed once again for me to keep them both at the 764th.

"Have them both transferred permanently to the 764th," Granny declared. "The paperwork just needs your signature, Doc!" (He finally called me "Doc," not captain.)

"Thanks anyway, again, men," Hewitt said, "but I've got to go back. You know those guys back there ain't had it as good as me and Paper the past few weeks. Paper means the world to them, too. He's not like other dogs. Once he gets to know you, he's like the family pet. On guard duty at night on patrol, Paper would go from one guy to the next to check on them. It was kind of like being at home. He's just a dog, but at least you could hug him and no one got jealous. Each guy would save some favorite piece of food to share with him."

"With Sherman's blood in him, he's going to be a real priss, now!" Dinky joked again.

"Hey, don't get me wrong," Hewitt retorted. "He'd be nice as a puppy around the guys he liked, but deadly as hell to the ones he didn't, especially the gooks – hated them worse than anything. One time, we were ordered into a village to do a little mopping up after a napalm bombing. Everything was pretty fried and they were pulling out the dead bodies from the VC bunkers. All of a sudden, out of this one, came this gook with his feet half burned off and this foot-long knife running for the first grunt he could see. Paper just leaped at him like a missile and ripped half his head away. The sucker never knew what hit him!" Hewitt concluded.

"Why don't one of you guys bring Sherman in here. I'll bet him and Paper have a few things to say to each other," I said.

"Yeah," said Tom. "We owe him as much as anybody!"

"I'll bet Paper saved your gonads more than once!" quipped J.B.

"Shoot, I don't know how any of the guys can function out there without a dog!" Hewitt stated.

"They all wanted one after seeing what Paper could do. I mean, he does his usual thing of finding booby traps; he's real good on anything with gun powder in it. And he's found a mess of enemy stashes of food and ammunition. And he's found a hell of a lot of tunnels. But besides all that, he seems to watch over my ass the best. I can't tell you how many times he's saved me from walking into those damn *punji* pits."

"A *punji* what?" asked J.B.

"You know," said Bell, those holes in the ground that the VC dig and place razor sharp bamboo spikes in them. Then they shit and piss on them and cover the hole with leaves."

"One nick from one of those spikes and you're out of action for a while! Maybe for good!" I added.

"I'd like to kiss that sergeant at Fort Benning that teamed me up with Paper!" Hewitt added.

"Did you get some of Sherman's blood, too?" Dink laughed.

"You'd better watch your mouth, now, Dink," I warned. "Paper is listening to every word."

Paper sat right with us, enjoying the bullshit, beer and pretzels along with Sherman.

"What was Paper's other kill?" asked Bell.

"It was just after leaving a village," Hewitt started, "and we were all pretty relaxed, thinking the worst was over. This gook came out of nowhere… just jumped up with a rifle. Paper was kind of low in the grass and this gook couldn't see him. Before he could get off a shot, Paper nailed his ass. By the time I got to him, he was shredded wheat. Paper weighs more than most of them. Let me get some pictures I took."

Hewitt left the room for a minute and came back with his duffel bag, started digging through it and produced a few photographs.

"Here are some of the guys waiting for us to get back if they ain't killed yet," Hewitt said, passing the pictures around.

"What's hanging around their necks?" asked Bell.

"Ears," replied Hewitt. "A lot of guys would cut off the gooks' ears and wear them around their neck. We figured if they were after our dogs' ears, we could play their games too!"

"How gross!" replied Porter.

I thought to myself, the bleeding hearts back home would have a field day with that kind of stuff. Everyone is always ready to criticize and condemn. But I wonder how many of them if placed under similar circumstances, would be able to even survive. We were all raised in a compassionate country by compassionate parents. Here, we were fighting an enemy where compassion wasn't a virtue, but an American weakness. They wouldn't think twice about booby-trapping one of their dead or even one of their live children. Each American had to cope with this new set of values just to stay alive.

We all shared our experiences, the good and the bad, and even had a few laughs. We talked most of the night and slept right on the floor in the surgery when we got tired. The next morning came all too quickly and the helicopter would be coming soon. Hewitt and Paper got ready. Hewitt had all his combat gear on and Paper obediently looked up at him.

"Look at that dog, Dink," I remarked. "I thought he'd always have a slight limp, but this morning I can hardly tell which leg is injured!"

It had been almost ten weeks to the day when Paper had come to us, barely alive, and now we were going to have to say goodbye to our two close friends. Tom could hear the beating of the helicopter blades in the distance that was almost echoing the pounding of our hearts. As I said before, I never liked goodbyes. Each guy lined up to take his turn saying goodbye and shaking hands.

"Kill a few for me!" snapped Bell.

"Give 'em hell!" poked J.B.

"Don't take any wooden nickels!" responded Granny.

"Good luck!" responded Snake.

"Keep your head down, Buddy!" Dow choked up.

Everyone gave Paper a hug and patted him on the head. Then, it was my turn. The helicopter was already landing outside the front gate of the compound. Hewitt and I stared at each other for a moment. A moment that was above any words we could say.

"Thanks again, Doc!" Hewitt smiled.

"Watch your ass!" I said. "And watch Paper's ass!"

I shook his hand and squeezed his shoulders. I could feel that old lump developing in my throat.

"And you watch Tom's ass, Paper!" I said. "And watch your own. Goodbye Paper Dog."

I gave Paper a long hug and hung onto him for as long as I could. The lump in my throat had finally sealed off any other words from leaving it. Hewitt ordered Paper to sit high (the command for Paper to sit up on his hind legs… the Army's salute for war dogs) and then Hewitt snapped to attention. I saluted them both. Hewitt ran to the chopper, Paper right at his side. From the helicopter door, he gave me the thumbs up and I stood there with both thumbs pointed up until they were both out of sight.

XVII.

No Greater Love

NONE OF US WHO REMAINED BEHIND could look at each other. One of us stood waving until the chopper was out of sight. Another kept yelling until they were no longer visible. The rest just stood quietly, but no one left until the Huey had completely disappeared. It at least gave me a chance for the lump in my throat to sink somewhat deeper and for my voice to return. I turned to Dinky, who was standing the closest.

"Congratulations, you did a fine job" I commended.

Then, in turn, I congratulated each one of them on a job well done. It was truly a team effort. Each man in his own way was responsible for this success. We had treated and performed other surgeries on many dogs and returned them to duty; but Paper, or should I say, Paper and Hewitt, were something special. We were just a team helping another team.

I knew all of us must have had the same feelings our parents had when they said goodbye to us as we left for Vietnam. There was worry… worry about your welfare and worry about the unknown. There were feelings of loss… the loss of a loved one that could very well be a permanent loss. There was that empty feeling… the feeling that the family wasn't whole, a vital part was missing. But whatever you tried to call the feeling, or describe it, we all felt lousy.

We went about the daily hospital routines as usual because we had to, but no one had much to joke about and everything seemed to require a lot more effort. None of us was quite there, but no one mentioned Hewitt or Paper. Everyone knew they were the only things on their minds, and no one wanted to talk about it. The only bright spot was seeing Major Kraft's face hit the floor when we told him that Paper had returned to duty.

Three days had passed since our goodbyes and we were back to doing something mundane on sick call that morning. I could never remember what it was when J.B. frantically came running into the treatment room.

"It's the phone, Doc, something about Paper! He's up in Da Nang. I think he's been shot!" J.B. shouted.

My heart dropped, as well as everything I was doing and I stampeded out of the hospital section and into the office area. The communication system in Vietnam left a lot to be desired, and to even make phone connections with Da Nang was very lucky. I raced frantically into my office and grabbed the phone with every man of the 764th right behind me.

"This is Captain Kubisz!" I shouted into the phone.

A faint distant crackling voice replied "You...... Paper......"

"REPEAT!" I yelled, at the top of my voice, "Is he OK?"

Then for a couple of seconds, the static cleared and I heard the words clearly, coldly and unmistakably...... the words that stopped my heart.

"He's dead, shot through the back of the head!"

I hesitated, almost in disbelief, and then asked apprehensively,

"Who's dead? Who got shot, Paper? Is Hewitt alright?"

Before the words were out of my mouth, the severe static and crackling interrupted and intensified.

"Ambush...... shot...... dead." The only words that I could understand and they echoed in my ears and brain. Then the line went completely silent. I shouted into it a few more times, hoping that the loudness alone would revive it, but nothing.

I slowly hung up the phone and looked at the faces staring blankly at me... J.B., Snake, Granny, Bell, and Dow. They already knew the worst..... Paper or Hewitt or both of them were dead. I sat there looking back and shaking my head negatively. Dink broke the silence.

"What happened?" he asked cautiously.

"The last words I heard were 'ambush... shot... dead!'"

"When I asked about Paper, I heard clearly, 'He's dead, shot through the back of the head!'"

I looked at Bell and Dow fighting back the tears. J.B. yelled and hit the wall. Porter went quickly to the other office and sat down. Terwillerger stood looking at the ground. I wanted to scream, to hit the walls or just plain cry. But I sat dumbfounded. The memories and pictures of Paper and Hewitt flooded my psyche like I was a drowning victim. Maybe I was the one to blame. It was my fault. Maybe I sent them back too soon. Why did I send them back in the first place? I could have kept them both until Hewitt's year in 'Nam was over. I became enraged with myself and the more I thought about it, the madder I got. My temper momentarily cleared the cobwebs and I broke the silent gloom.

"Alright! Damn it!" I shouted. "Dinky get your travelin' gear and rear and catch the next plane to Da Nang. Granny, cut some orders for Dink to fly up there and find out what the hell happened. Maybe Hewitt's alright. Bell, get the jeep and drive Dow to the air base and get him on the next plane headed that way, top priority!" I ordered.

Dink was on his way. I don't think any of us said a word the rest of the day. Each man was alone with his thoughts and imagination of what might have happened. I thought about the voice over the phone saying, "shot... back of head..." How could he get shot in the back of the head unless he walked into an ambush? If they depended on Paper too much, maybe he led them into an ambush and they all got wiped out? Maybe I kept them too long and Paper forgot his training or got careless? Why in the hell did I send them back? The emotions inside were overcoming reason. I slammed my fist straight into the wall!

There was a lot of that kind of stuff that day. Once in a while, you'd hear "damn" or "hell" or "fuck" and someone hitting the wall. Nobody ate lunch or dinner. Each of us kept to ourselves, trying to handle the news and emotions the best we could, hoping to hear the phone ring and hear some good news from Da Nang. Maybe I heard one or two words wrong. I tried a few times to connect on the phone, but all the lines were dead.

The following morning, we stood in the breezeway like washed-out zombies, staring down the long gravel road that led to the 764th, waiting for a glimpse of a truck or jeep with Dink returning. Our eyes were red from lack of sleep or from crying. Maybe we could hear the sounds of an approaching helicopter bringing Paper and Hewitt back to us, like ten weeks ago. But nothing moved for almost the whole morning. It was like the entire 764th and the surrounding area stopped functioning. Then in the distance, a faint cloud of dust signaled the approach of a jeep.

We all stood shoulder to shoulder at the gate. It was Dinky. He must have hitched a ride from the air base because our phone lines were down. I strained my eyes to see him, to get some hint of what happened before he even got to us. As the jeep got closer, I could make out his expression and it told me the news I already expected; it wasn't good. The jeep slowly pulled up and Dink somberly stepped out, grabbing his duffle bag. He thanked his ride and looked at all of us, with that look that tells you the worst before you ask, and are afraid to ask.

"Is Hewitt OK, Dink?" I asked cautiously.

"He's fine," was the slow, welcomed reply, "except for the loss of Paper."

"Paper's dead, huh Dink?" asked J.B., still not accepting that he was killed.

Dink nodded affirmatively and walked, shoulders bent and head down, towards the hospital and into the large office area. I told him to sit down and tell us the whole story. We sat around him like children waiting to hear a fairytale.

He told us that a week before Hewitt and Paper returned, the Americal Division stationed in the Ia Drang Valley was nearly wiped out. It came close to a defeat for our side in this war. As soon as Paper and Hewitt returned, they were already making plans to retake the Ia Drang Valley using the 101st Airborne, because they could get in quickly. They had been working the nearby Ashau Valley. Several companies of the 101st were airlifted in, including Paper and Tom. One of the companies landed in a large number of VC and immediately got completely cut off from the rest and were surrounded. The closest unit to them had Hewitt and Paper. They were ordered to help the trapped company as soon as possible, to spare nothing and throw caution to the wind. The situation was desperate, but with a dog like Paper, they could move fast... just follow his lead and keep going. The trapped unit was about five miles away.

Paper was leading the way about 150 yards ahead of Hewitt and was crossing a ravine with a stream running through it. He got up on the other side. They were almost in range of the other company when Paper alerted. Hewitt made him get down and Paper crawled all the way back to him and alongside him and laid his head over Tom's neck like he was trying to protect him. Tom then motioned for the advancing company to move up and when the VC ambush ahead knew that they were detected, all hell broke loose for a few seconds before the VC retreated into the jungle. Hewitt reached back to pet and thank Paper again, but his hand felt blood at the back of Paper's head. He grabbed him, but he just lay limp in his arms. Paper's massive head was the only thing that could have stopped a bullet meant for Hewitt. No one else was even wounded. They got to the other company that was surrounded just in time to save them all.

"Hewitt refused to leave Paper and carried him back all the way to Da Nang. Some vet up there pronounced him dead, but Hewitt insisted that he call you first," Dow continued. "He told them that we could bring Paper back from the dead. We did it before!" He smiled slightly.[1]

"How is he?" I asked.

Dinky shrugged his shoulders. "I don't know if he'll ever be the same. But, you know he's tough. He'll be alright." Dow concluded.

Hewitt had saved Paper's life ten weeks before and now Paper had paid the ultimate price for the life of his friend, Tom. They would no longer have to worry about future goodbyes or what would happen to them later. They said their final goodbyes in private, alone with each other. Paper gave his life for his friend and for the men of the 101st Airborne. Their families wouldn't have to say the final goodbye to their sons.

"It's too bad the Army doesn't give medals to the war dogs," I said. "Paper would be up for the Congressional Medal of Honor!"

We all felt like we should give him something… something to present to Hewitt for recognition. So, we all chipped in and bought a walnut plaque with a brass plate inscription. It read:

This is dedicated to the scout dog named Paper of the 101st Airborne.
He gave his life so that others could live.
We loved him and we'll never forget him.
The Men of the Fightin' 764th Medical Detachment

| Doc | J.B. | Dinky |
| Granny | Ding Dong | Snake |

So that was Paper's destiny. And everything we did, and everything that Paper and Hewitt had to go through, had some meaning. Unlike a fairytale, many war stories have a sad ending, but deep inside, we knew it could end no other way. None of us will ever forget Paper and Hewitt. Paper Dog will live on forever in our memories and now in this book.

1. Official military records state Paper's date for being killed in action (KIA) as 06/26/1969.

EPILOGUE

BY THE TIME TOM AND PAPER went back to duty, most of the men of the 764th were getting short. Bell and J.B. were the first to go, followed by Dow and Granny and then Terwillerger. Their replacements were okay I guess, but somehow they never fit or replaced any of the Dirty Half Dozen. Terwilliger went on to head the reptile department at the Cincinnati Zoo. The last time I heard from Bell, he was working at a military base in Maryland. I couldn't find any of the others even with the Army records (Dow, J.B. or Granny).

The major and the colonel waited like vultures for me to leave so they could take over the 764th and make it part of the 176th. At least I have the distinction of being the last C.O. of the 764th. Ray Holmgren, the first C.O., set up practice in Portland, Oregon with his wife Penny and raised two sons. After Vietnam, the eruption of Mount St. Helens was just another day for Ray. Dusty Dussel and Jack Crawford returned to Texas and started practices. Bob Eilert (our skin graft specialist) went on to head a children's hospital in Colorado.

I was the last to go and I still had one more goodbye to make... Lee.

Both of us knew that the day would come when we would have to return to our own worlds. Lee wouldn't be happy in the United States and I couldn't stay in Vietnam. We shared a very special love and we shared a little part of each other's lives. I know that people in the "real world" find this kind of relationship kind of different. Lee was a survivor and I can only hope that she and her little boy are safe and happy.

The day I boarded the plane for home, she said her goodbyes to me at the airbase. I looked out the plane's window and saw her standing there with one of my men from the 764th who drove us to the base. I was flooded with emotions – Lee, Paper, Tom, the 764th. I sat there sobbing like a baby.

The guy next to me put his hand on my shoulder.

"It's alright. It's all over now. We're going home," he said.

I stared at the floor. "It will never be over."

When I returned to the States, everyone thought I had changed and that I was too quiet. They were right. I had changed, but only for the better. All my experiences had a very positive effect on me. Before I went to Vietnam, I think I was materialistic and placed more importance on getting a sports car than I did on personal relationships. 'Nam taught me the things that are really important in life. As far as being quiet, I think one reason why most guys were so quiet is that they were afraid to open their mouths and say some four-letter obscenity. A year and a half of mostly male companionship can turn you just a little above caveman.

I had a hard time establishing any kind of relationship with the girls when I got back. I found most of them extremely shallow, with no idea of the important things in life. But, when I gave up trying, the right girl came into my life who wanted the same things I did. We were married for twenty-five years and raised four handsome, talented sons: John, Josh, Jake and James. They gave me all the excitement I needed. I've tried to raise them with the same principles that my parents instilled in me, but also the values I learned in Vietnam... that all living things have a value and that all life is very precious. I have ten grandchildren and I'm still practicing today.

I know it was harder for Hewitt to come back to the real world, and I know a lot of guys never will. But Tom was lucky to meet the right girl, Joan. They raised two beautiful daughters, Rachel and Megan. For a while, they raised and trained rare and exotic tropical birds in Florida. Of course, he trained dogs for protection in the private sector.

I have to add one more thing to this story. In August 2019, I attended a Vietnam veteran reunion in Kokomo, Indiana. I only attended one before about thirty years ago, and I wasn't planning to attend this one. Ron Werneth, a very good author in his own right, convinced me to attend. A few years ago, Ron got interested in the war dogs' story and has compiled a great deal of information on the dogs and their handlers. I consider him a good friend and told him that I would meet him there. I wasn't expecting the large number of veterans who turned out and I certainly wasn't expecting to meet anyone from fifty years ago. Within minutes, someone walked up to me.

"I know you don't remember me. We are both a lot older," he started.

"I remember you."

"What's was your dog's name?" I asked.

"Rebel," he replied.

I smiled. "I do remember, Rebel. Do you know how I remember him? He was the best damn dog I have ever seen at running an obstacle course!"

His face came to life with a big smile. "You do remember him! He could run the course and never stop' til I told him to!"

"Whatever happened to him?" I asked.

"He was killed in action," he lamented.

"FUCK!" I blurted out.

Everyone around us turned and looked. Some were ladies and I apologized for my vulgarity, but they all nodded and said they understood. We must never forget the contributions these dogs made. Every one of them had a story and they were all very special. Together they saved an estimated 10,000 lives. After I attended the Vietnam Memorial Wall in Washington D.C., I pictured a statue of a war dog at the entrance, still guarding the departed. I could see Paper with his cast and bandages on. I met several handlers from that era and was waiting at the War Memorial for the customary group photo. I felt a tap on my shoulder. I turned around and there was a guy about my age and a younger man about the age of my youngest son, James (about thirty).

"Yes, sir, you are the guy, a little older and grayer, but you're him. You saved my dog's life and that dog saved mine. More importantly, this is my son!"

I extended my hand and shook his son's hand. "Be proud of your dad for serving in Vietnam,"

"I am, sir. I love him," his son replied.

I looked at the veteran, his eyes filled with tears. How or what could anyone say at that moment? I didn't get his name or even remember saying goodbye. In an instant, he and his son disappeared. I took the photo. I knew I wasn't smiling. I said a quick goodbye to Ron Werneth and went to my car. I couldn't talk about my experiences for days. Maybe I helped to save this handler's dog but I know that I didn't do it alone. The Men of the Fightin' 764th must be given the credit. I hope the ones that are left are reading this.

In 1999, Hollywood premiered an excellent documentary on the war dogs. Paper's story was included.

I talked to Tom Hewitt just the other day. He's doing fine. We talked about Paper Dog like it was yesterday.

Right: Hard to believe I've been a veterinarian for over 50 years! Here I am circa 1979 at Argonne Animal Hospital in Lemont, Illinois.

Below: My three sons. Left to right: Jacob, James and Joshua. Jake and Josh are twins.

*Howard County
Vietnam Veterans'
Reunion in Kokomo,
Indiana, 2019. With
military historian Ron
Werneth and retired
MWD Brutusz.*

Printed in the USA
CPSIA information can be obtained
at www.ICGtesting.com
LVHW010204071223
765929LV00026B/183/J